The Augustan Repr

THE
MASTER MERCURY

[DANIEL DEFOE]
(1704)

Introduction by
Frank H. Ellis
and
Henry L. Snyder

Publication Number *184*

WILLIAM ANDREWS CLARK MEMORIAL LIBRARY

University of California, Los Angeles

1977

GENERAL EDITORS
William E. Conway, William Andrews Clark Memorial Library
George Robert Guffey, University of California, Los Angeles
Maximillian E. Novak, University of California, Los Angeles
David Stuart Rodes, University of California, Los Angeles

ADVISORY EDITORS
James L. Clifford, Columbia University
Ralph Cohen, University of Virginia
Vinton A. Dearing, University of California, Los Angeles
Arthur Friedman, University of Chicago
Louis A. Landa, Princeton University
Earl Miner, Princeton University
Samuel H. Monk, University of Minnesota
Everett T. Moore, University of California, Los Angeles
Lawrence Clark Powell, William Andrews Clark Memorial Library
James Sutherland, University College, London
H. T. Swedenberg, Jr., University of California, Los Angeles
Robert Vosper, William Andrews Clark Memorial Library

CORRESPONDING SECRETARY
Beverly J. Onley, William Andrews Clark Memorial Library

EDITORIAL ASSISTANT
Frances M. Reed, University of California, Los Angeles

INTRODUCTION

In the *Review* for 12 August 1704 Defoe complained about the "Addition of four New Papers added this Week to the Throng of Nonsence, with which the Town was plagu'd before." This is Swift's joke in *A Tale of a Tub* (April 1704):

> *For a Man to set up for a Writer, when the Press swarms with, &c.*[1]

Swift's joke, however, is directed against cousin Dryden, while Defoe's is directed against himself. It is this kind of self-irony that endears Defoe to his readers today.

One of the new recruits to "the Throng of Nonsence" was *The Master Mercury*, a newspaper of which Defoe published the first number on 8 August 1704. In the second number, published on 10 August 1704 but misdated 8 August, the author of *The Master Mercury* jeered at the author of the *Review*:

> who can forbear [he said] letting the Author of the *Review* know somebody knows something as well as himself.[2]

The author of the *Review* replied by putting the author of *The Master Mercury* on the agenda of The Scandal. Club:

> the Club could not but take notice of one of the New Gentlemen Authors, call'd *the Master-Mercury,* and observing that he appears in the World with a very great Stock of Assurance ... and abundance of great Things which he promises to do, bidding bold Defyance to all the World.[3]

Nor could Defoe finish without getting in a plug for *A Hymn to the Pillory* which had been written in Newgate and sold on the streets while its author stood in the pillory on 29 July 1703, and for *A Hymn to Victory* that had been written after its author's release from Newgate and was now ready for the press:

— i —

> [but] if he will be obstinate [in his stated intention to make "Plain and Impartial Reflections" on all other newspapers], then they [the Scandal. Club] Counsel him to have always by him, ready for the Press, a *HYMN,* &c.[4]

Defoe's willingness to identify himself as "Mr. *Review*" and his concealment of himself as *"the Master-Mercury"* make a remarkable contrast. Also worth remarking are the high spirits in which he undertook *The Master Mercury.*

It has long been known that Defoe was *capable* of writing two or even three newspapers at the same time, but until the discovery of the apparently unique run of *The Master Mercury* in the Yale University Library,[5] it was not known that he was doing so in August and September 1704. His purposes in undertaking a second biweekly newspaper are almost unfathomable. "The Thread of this Undertaking must describe it self," as Defoe said, much less truthfully, of the *Review*.[6]

Defoe's purposes in the *Review* may be inferred from his letters to Robert Harley, principal secretary of state in Godolphin's reshuffled ministry, and from the *Review* itself. The overt propaganda theme is the familiar wartime slogan: Know your Enemy. "The very Center and Heart of my Design," Defoe said, is to expound the causes and effects of the *grandeur* of France under Louis XIV.[7] So successful was he in this effort that he was accused of "favouring the *French* Interest, and being bought and brib'd with *French* Money."[8] Godolphin professed to be shocked. "This magnifying of France," he told Harley, "is a thing so odious ... that I can't think any jury would acquit this man if discovered."[9] Harley, who supplied the money for the *Review* out of secret service funds, did not change the propaganda theme, but Defoe devoted the next issue to a defense of "this particular Article of Magnifying the *French* Power."[10]

Defoe explained the *Review* to himself as "writing a History sheet by sheet" or "Writing a History by Inches."[11] And he justified the *Review* to himself in the way that art is commonly justified: as "exact information of how to rearrange one's psyche in order to anticipate the next blow from our own extended faculties," in Marshall McLuhan's words, or as "instruction in defense," in Harold Bloom's phrase.[12] Defoe himself called it "The unquestioned Benefit to this Nation of seeing our Danger, and of knowing the worst of our Difficulties."[13]

Defoe justified the *Review* to himself by calling it "History," but he also knew that history is "Tedious." So to each number of the *Review* after the first he added a *"Mercure Scandale:* Or, Advice from the Scandalous Club," to "wheedle" the public into reading the "History."[14] This formula — Know your Enemy *plus* scandal — was so successful that some numbers of the *Review* had to be reprinted, and there was soon a demand for more frequent publication.[15]

But the formula proved unresponsive to the real purpose of the *Review*. Defoe's repeated boast that neither the history of France nor the scandal allowed "meddling with State Affairs" (i.e., party politics) was in fact a complaint.[16] For the real purpose of the *Review* was to subserve and prolong the ministry of Godolphin and Harley. The ministry's policy of divide and conquer – "Peace at Home" was the slogan – meant splitting both parties and gathering in the "Moderate Men of both Partyes."[17]

"This Moderation," as Defoe perceived, "is a very ambiguous Phrase."[18] And this was one of its advantages in propaganda. It could denote the coalition government of Godolphin and Harley. Yet its connotations were wide enough to include the Revolution Settlement, toleration of dissenters, and the Hanoverian succession. Conversely, the opposition could easily be set down as "Immoderation Display'd."

The intractability of the Know your Enemy *plus* scandal formula and the *need* of "meddling with State Affairs" may be one of the reasons Defoe undertook *The Master Mercury*. "This Moderation is a very ambiguous Phrase," he wrote in the second number of *The Master Mercury*, "and perhaps," he added, "we may have Occasion to make frequent use of it in these Papers." The length of the *Review* may have been another reason. The original *Review*. was a quarto pamphlet of eight pages. But after four numbers Defoe was required to economize. "It is not for want of Matter wherewith to Entertain the World," he said in the *Review* of 18 March 1704, "that this Paper is thus reduc'd from a whole to half a Sheet." *The Master Mercury* restored the cut.

Defoe may have thought of *The Master Mercury* as a supplement to the *Review*. There was already a tradition of newspaper supplements. Samuel Buckley's *The Daily Courant* had "Supplements" Edward Jones added "Expresses" to *The London Gazette.* And the French-language *Leiden Gazette* published *Supplements aux Novelles Extraordinaires.* It was advertized in the *Review* for 23 September 1704 that "Once every Month, there will be Printed a Suppliment,"[19] and two days later appeared the last known number of *The Master Mercury.* The timing suggests that *The Master Mercury* was the first of a series of supplements to the *Review.*

It is possible that Defoe started *The Master Mercury* without Harley's knowledge. "In all my Writing," he claimed ten years later, "I ever capitulated [i.e., contracted] for my Liberty to speak according to my own Judgment of Things."[20] And James Sutherland has even suggested that "So far from dictating a policy to any one, Harley was constantly looking around for suggestions as to what he ought to do next .... On the evidence it seems probable that Defoe influenced the Minister quite as much as the Minister brought pressure to bear on him to write against his conscience."[21] There is plenty of evidence in the *Review,* however, that Defoe felt constrained by the Know your Enemy *plus* scandal formula.[22] In *The Master Mercury* he attacked some of his favorite targets: stock market manipulators, Jacobites, and the judges who so unjustly sentenced him for publishing *The Shortest Way with the Dissenters* (December 1702). And there is plenty of evidence that Defoe concealed from Harley the authorship of some of his writing.[23] So he may have started *The Master Mercury* "to speak according to [his] own Judgment of Things." But this is only speculation.

Defoe had good reasons, both personal and political, to attack Sir George Rooke. While he was still in Newgate, his lawyer, William Colepeper, had been assaulted in the street and challenged to fight by hired bravoes working for Sir George. Once he was out of Newgate, one of Defoe's first exercises for Harley was an essay, "Of The Fleet and Sir Geo: Rook," demanding removal from his post as admiral of the English fleet of "this Obnoxious Suspected Man" who had successfully avoided an engagement with the French fleet in six campaigns since May 1692.[24] Harley did not allow this essay to be published, but Defoe slipped a few phrases from it into the *Review.*[25] On 18 August 1704 Defoe published *A True State of* the *Difference between Sir George Rook, Knt. and William Colepeper, Esq.*, a detailed exposé of Sir George's cowardice and its consequences.[26] Three days later he resumed the attack on Sir George in *The Master Mercury*. "Who dare say Sir G.R. won't fight?" he asked and then went on to recall a recent occasion when Sir George would not fight:

> at *Cadiz* . . . it was thought fit rather to Land at Port St. *Maries*, where there was good Booty to be had, then boldly at once to venture upon the Town it self and knock our heads against Stone Walls.[27]

If he had not know it beforehand, Harley could have learned on 26 September 1704, from at least two manuscript newsletters, that Defoe was writing *The Master Mercury*. One reported that "Daniel de Foe," whom Harley knew to be in East Anglia "Spreading Principles of Temper, Moderation, and Peace" as Harley's confidential agent, had been "ordered to be taken into custody for reflecting on admiral Rooke, in his Master Mercury, whereby he has forfeited his recognizance for his good behaviour."[28] Harley knew that no such order had been issued, but he may not have known that Defoe was writing *The Master Mercury*.

What had started the rumor is presumably the issue of 21 September, and not that of 21 August. On 13/24 August Rooke had fought, or avoided fighting as the case may be, the battle of Málaga and the whole town was singing, to the tune *Hey boys up go we*,

> As brave Sir *George*, *Thoulouse* did beat,
>   So brave *Thoulouse* beat him; . . .
> They both did fight, they both were beat,
>   They both did run away;
> They both did strive again to meet
>   The quite contrary way.[29]

The Master Mercury of 21 September 1704 "reflecting" on the battle of Málaga is very carefully written to avoid another prosecution for seditious libel. Defoe's strategy is to keep repeating "we have had a great Victory . . . as Signal a Victory as this Nation every received . . . it is a very great Victory . . . a

Victory ... Victory to the *English*... If this was not a Victory I know not what can deserve the name of it ... It is a Victory," but to interpolate details that call into question Rooke's judgment, loyalty, and personal bravery.[30]

On 28 September 1704 Defoe wrote to Harley from Bury St. Edmunds about a similar report in a manuscript newsletter by Joseph Fox. "I am surpriz'd to find my Name in the Written News Letters of this day," he said, "as Taken into Custody, and Comitted by her Majtes Order for Ill Treating Sir Geo: Rook."[31] Since Harley had vetoed "Of The Fleet and Sir Geo: Rook" and may not have known about *The Master Mercury,* Defoe was extremely apprehensive. In his guilty imagination he grovels at Harley's feet; "It Can Not be, that I Can be Guilty of any Thing to Displease you ....I ... was Comeing Up Post to Thro' my Self at your feet ... If I were Guilty of high Treason a Letter ... should Cause me To Come and Put my Self into your Power."[32]

Apparently all that Harley demanded was a formal retraction, for on 7 October 1704 the Scandal. Club decided that "'tis Scandalous, that the Debate, whether 'tis a Victory or no, should be set on Foot in *England*... when the Government has declar'd their Opinion, that it is an Action Glorious to Her Majesty's Arms."[33] Defoe knew that government "Opinion" does not make victories, but by this time *The Master Mercury* had ceased publication

Smith College
and
The University of Kansas

NOTES TO THE INTRODUCTION

1. Jonathan Swift, *A Tale of a Tub, With Other Early Works, 1696-1707,* ed. Herbert Davis (Oxford: Basil Blackwell, 1957), p. 27.

2. *The Master Mercury,* [10] August 1704 (p. 5).

3. *Review,* 12 August 1704 (I, 200).

4. *Ibid.* For Defoe to call himself *"the Master-Mercury"* is both pretentious and self-deprecating: pretentious because Mercury is the god of eloquence, and self-deprecating because a mercury was a vendor of broadsides (in addition to the references in *OED,* see *An Elegy on the Death of the Author of the Characters, &c. Of the Ladies Invention* [n.d., but May 1699], of which the first line is, "He's Dead! Lament ye Mercuries and Hawkers"). So *"the Master-Mercury"* is king of the news butchers.

5. A query seeking other locations for *The Master Mercury* remains unanswered (Frank H. Ellis, "Defoe and *The Master Mercury,*" *N&Q,* 217 [January 1972], 28-29). One number, *The Master Mercury,* 18 September 1704, was known to be in the British Library, but was not suspected to be by Defoe (William T. Morgan and Chloe Siner Morgan, *A Bibliography of British History (1700-1715),* 5 vols. [Bloomington: Indiana University Press, 1934-42], III [1939], 284).

6. *Review,* 12 August 1704 (I, 197).

7. *Review,* 1 August 1704 (I, 186).

8. *Review,* 4 July 1704 (I, 154).

9. Historical Manuscripts Commission, *Calendar of the Manuscripts of the Marquis of Bath Preserved at Longleat, Wiltshire,* 3 vols. (London: H. M. Stationery Office, 1904-08), I (1904), 59; hereafter cited as *HMC Bath MSS.*

10. *Review,* 4 July 1704 (I, 153).

11. *Review,* 4 April 1704 (I, 49), 4 July 1704 (I, 153).

12. Marshall MacLuhan, *Understanding Media, The Extensions of Man* (New York: McGraw-Hill, 1965), p. 66; Harold Bloom, "The use of poetry," *New York Times* (12 November 1975), p. 41.

13. *Review,* 4 April 1704 (I, 49). The importance of this idea for Defoe may be judged by the frequency and the length of interval with which he repeats it; cf. "my own Countrymen, to whom I have shewn their Danger, and whom I have endeavour'd to wake out of their Sleep" *(Review,* 4 July 1704

[I,155]); "I have told you where your Danger lies. ...I care not how much my Noise offends you, for I write to please none of you, but to awaken you" (*Review*, 11 November 1712, [IX] 59).

14. *A Supplementary Journal, To the Advice from the Scandal. Club; For the Month of September, 1704*, p. 5. Readers objected so violently to the affectation of *"Mercure Scandale"* and to the solecism of *"Scandalous Club"* that the final form became "Advice from the Scandal. Club," with the full stop standing as Defoe's defiance of petty grammarians.

15. *Review*, 15 July 1704 (I, 168). The demand for more frequent publication (*Review*, 30 May 1704 [I, 116]) was not met for another year (*Review*, 22 March 1705 [II, 29]). Thereafter, until the last number on 11 June 1713, the *Review* was a tri-weekly.

16. *Review*, 6 May 1704 (I, 87), 10 June 1704 (I, 127), 7 October 1704 (I, 263).

17. *The Letters of Daniel Defoe*, ed. George Harris Healey (Oxford: Clarendon Press, 1955), p. 53; hereafter cited as Defoe, *Letters*.

18. *The Master Mercury*, [10] August 1704 (p. 7).

19. Five of these, entitled *A Supplementary Journal to the Advice from the Scandal. Club* and dated September 1704-January 1705, were published between 21 October 1704 and 3 May 1705 (*Review*, 21 October 1704 [I, 279], 1 May 1705 [II, 100]). These were succeeded on 6 June 1705 by *The Little Review*, published weekly for 23 numbers.

20. Daniel Defoe, *An Appeal to Honour and Justice* (1715), p. 21.

21. James Sutherland, *Defoe* (Philadelphia: Lippincott, 1938), p. 107.

22. *Review*, 13, June 1704 (I, 131), 17 June 1704 (I, 134), 20 June 1704 (I, 137), 24 June 1704 (I, 142).

23. *Poems on Affairs of State*, ed. George deF. Lord et al., 7 vols. (New Haven: Yale University Press. 1963-75), VI (1970), 632, VII (1975), 463, 493; hereafter cited as *POAS* (Yale).

24. Defoe, *Letters*, pp. 20, 25. By a kind of antonomasia, Defoe reduces Rooke to a common noun with a variety of meanings: *"Rakes,* or *R*[ooke]*s" (The Master Mercury*, [10] August 1704 [p. 7]; "Rookites" [highflying Tories] (Defoe, *Letters*, p. 61); "this Bully Magistrate [Sir Salathiel Lovell] ...this R[oo]ke" *(A Supplementary Journal, to the Advice from the Scandal. Club; For the Month of September, 1704*, p. 13).

25. "The french Admirall...Ventur'd into the Mediteranean with 29 Sail" (Defoe, *Letters*, p. 21); "Count *de Tholouse,* with 29 [sail] ventured to follow into the *Mediterranean*" (*Review*, 24 June 1704 [I, 141]); "at Bar-

celona ... Monstrous .... To Land a Force Inferiour to the Enemy" (Defoe, *Letters*, pp. 22-23): "like Landing 3500 Men at *Barcelona*" (*Review*, 24 June 1704 [I, 142]); "with a Force Very Superior .... Why Did We Not Fight them" (Defoe, *Letters*, pp. 21-22): *"Tholouse*... in vain, endeavour'd to fight the Confederate Fleet" (*Review*, 24 June 1704 [I, 141]). Rooke quit his post in December 1704 (Narcissus Luttrell, *A Brief Historical Relation of State Affairs from September 1678 to April 1714*, 6 vols. [Oxford: 1857], V [1857], 505; hereafter cited as Luttrell).

26. The preface is signed "William Colepeper," but Charles Leslie understood that it was written by *"Legion"* and "Carefully *Advertis'd* and *Re-Advertis'd* in the Papers of our *Scandalous Club*, such as *Observator, Review*, &c." *(The Rehearsal of Observator,* 30 September-7 October 1704). *A True State* was advertized in the *Review* of 22 August, 26 August, 2 September, 5 September, 9 September, 12 September, 26 September, 7 October and in *The Master Mercury* of 11 September, 14 September, 21 September, 25 September. Since no copies of *The Master Mercury*, 23 August-7 September, are known, this record may be incomplete.

27. *The Master Mercury*, 21 August 1704 (p. 19). Defoe also wrote a poem on this debacle (*POAS* [Yale], VI, 467-484).

28. Defoe, *Letters*, p. 60; Luttrell, V, 469. Attribution of *The Master Mercury* to Defoe was made in another manuscript newsletter preserved in the Newdigate Collection at the Folger Shakespeare Library (LC 2799). In this letter dated 30 September 1704 it is reported that "Mr. De ffoe the Author of a halfe sheet of Paper Published twice a Week Entituled the Master Mercury is silenced for a Blasphemous Expression in it and Ordered to be prosecuted for that and for Reflecting on Sr. George Rook and the late sea fight." If this report had been true it would have ended Defoe's new career as Harley's confidential agent. Defoe's sentence for writing *The Shortest Way with the Dissenters* required him to provide security for his good behavior for seven years and there had been speculation in the press about who had paid the money ([William Pittis], *Heraclitus Ridens*, 2-6 November 1703). So the ministry's investment in Defoe would have been lost if he had been arrested on another libel charge (Historical Manuscripts Commission, *The Manuscripts of the Duke of Portland*, 10 vols. (London: H. M. Stationery Office, 1891-1931), IV (1897), 75; hereafter cited as *HMC Portland MSS*.). Defoe, *Letters*, p. 58, n. 4 should read *"The Master Mercury*, 21 September 1704" instead of "the *Review* for 22 Aug."; p. 65, n. 1 should read *"The Address"* (*POAS* [Yale], VI, 631) instead of *"Legion's Humble Address to the Lords."*

29. *POAS* (Yale), VII, 15-18. Godolphin complained to Harley that "Our sea victory not proving true makes the discourse of that matter very disagreeable" (*HMC Bath MSS.*, I, 62). In spite of the facts, the government decided to call it a great victory (Luttrell, V, 470).

30. Here is an example of Defoe's rhetoric. English naval tactics prohibited

firing except at close range. In a minor engagement in the Channel that summer Captain T. Butler brought the *Worcester* so close to an interloping Swedish man-of-war "that our yardarms were within one another" before ordering "our whole broadside to be fired into him" (*HMC Portland MSS.,* VIII, 134). Rooke on the other hand exhausted his ammunition in long-range firing at the French fleet (*HMC Bath MSS.,* I, 62; Gilbert Burnet, *History of His Own Time,* 2 vols. [London, 1724-34], II [1734], 390). So when Defoe says, "The Admiral ...could not get up so near them as he intended," the effect is wholly comic (*The Master Mercury,* 21 September 1704 [p. 55]).

31. John Dyer and Joseph Fox (Henry R. Plomer, *A Dictionary of the Printer and Booksellers... from 1668 to 1725* [Oxford: Oxford University Press, 1922], p. 120) are said to have written the offending newsletters in the advertizement that Defoe inserted in the *Review,* 4 November and 7 November 1704, exposing the whole story as a fabrication undertaken *"to bring him into Trouble."*

32. Defoe, *Letters,* pp. 59-60.

33. *Review,* 7 October 1704 (I, 263).

BIBLIOGRAPHICAL NOTE

The facsimile of *The Master Mercury* (8 August-25 September 1704) is reproduced from the copy (Shelf Mark: Z17/219d) in the Beinecke Library, Yale University. Of the fifteen numbers, 3 and 6-10 are lacking. Pages 45-48 are misnumbered 41-44, respectively, and page 50 is misnumbered 40. This unique surviving run of *The Master Mercury* is in very poor condition; contrary to ARS policy, the dark backgrounds of the photographic reproductions have been retained to provide a better sense of that condition and in order to make incomplete words near the edges of the leaves more decipherable.

THE
Master Mercury:

BEING

A Faithful ABSTRACT of all the NEWS both Foreign and Domestick.

With Plain and Impartial Reflections both on Persons and Things. Particularly on Mr. *Lloyd*'s *St. Helena* Letter.

Tuesday, August 8. 1704.

THAT Printing of Papers is become a Publick Nusance, I believe will be granted by all People; and the Author of this may be supposed to take an odd way of curing the Evil, by encreasing the Number.

And yet if suitable Encouragement be given to his honest Design, perhaps in Time he may bring this Paper to be equivolent to all the News Papers in the Town.

He hopes no body will find fault with his Title, and he undertakes to tell the World he will answer for it, the Subject shall agree, for there shall be Reflection enough.

If he observes the *Observator*, or reviews the *Review*, if he tells the *Daily Courant*, when he writes a great deal of *no News*, and consequently picks our Pockets, if he taxes their Sense that can bear to read the *London Post*, or their Judgments that believe the *Flying Post*, if he tells the *Post Boy* he has a better Stock of Im——— than Intelligence, if he charges the *Post Man* with Bombast and Tautology, 'tis hop'd those Gentlemen Authors will endeavour to mend or defend, if neither of these shall be the Consequence, this Paper will descend to more effectual Methods, as follows.

When the *London Post* talks Nonsense, we may endeavour to make it intelligible; when Mr. R——path being busy spoiling the *Monthly Mercury*, writes 13 for 12 in the *Flying Post*, we'll endeavour to set the Readers to rights; if *Abel R--r* happens to stretch a Point in the *Post Boy*, we'll open the Matter; if the *Post Man* rumbles in the Clouds, we'll put him into *English* a little, and help the *Frenchman* to talk of his own Country Affairs; if the *Daily Courant* commits daily Mistakes, we must help him to translate *French* Nonsense, and put it into *English* Sense; if the *Observator* be impudent, we'll rub him with his own Towel; nay, if even the *Review* begins to hunt counter, and forget himself, he must excuse us if we bring him before his own Club.

[2]

...d yet the Undertakers of this Paper desire the Reader to observe that we shall not take up their Time with the little and insignificant Labour of correcting the News Men, we freely remit that Task to the scandalous Club-men. But as we shall make Reflections upon Foreign and Domestick Affairs, the Editors of our large Accounts must come a-cross us of Course.

In this Paper therefore, the Reader will find the Publick Affairs duly, and as succinctly as possible, related from the best Intelligence, and so in the reading of this Paper, the World shall be supplyed with all the material News, tho' in this perhaps we may not out-go our Neighbours. But as every Article shall have its necessary and just Observations, which we find in some not at all attempted, and in others very lamely performed; in this Part we hope to give the World some Helps, please them both by Instruction and Diversion, and perhaps may say something, which no body says but our selves.

When there is no News in Town, and 3 or 4 Mails due, the Reader shall never find the Paper fill'd up with long Speeches of Ambassadors, and vain Repetitions of forgotten Stories, *a la mode a Postman*; the Letter of the Print will never be altered from a small to a great *a la mode a Courant* for want of *somewhat to say*. But when there is least News possibly we may have most Business.

And yet we shall not have the Face to imitate the *Daily Courant*, to come out every Day, but we hope to have our Paper rather enquired for, than to glut the World with a daily Breakfast as if they wanted an Antidote every Morning to keep out the infectious Air of News-mongers Impertinence.

In short, without more Apology, we depend for the Success of this Paper upon *its own proper Merit*: we expect

it should be thrown by at first, as a new Thing, good for little. We come out at a Season of the Year, when the Town is empty of People, but full of *Pen and Ink*, but we pretend to force our way by the prevailing Power of our just Performance, and shall always undertake to furnish the Reader with something both pleasant and profitable.

This first Paper comes happily out at an Interval of News; we had Yesterday 3 Mails due from *Holland*, and the Winds hang still out of the Way; and yet 'tis to be observ'd, and we cannot but think it worth every bodies Notice, that our News Papers find something to be paid for.

The preposterous Nonsence of a Man printing a News Paper every Day, when all People know there has been no Foreign News this ten Days, and that he can have nothing say, but what Fragments he must pick out of the Papers almost a Fortnight old, affords us this noted Speculation, how easy this Town is to be imposed upon.

'Tis confest, he that is willing to have his Pocket pick'd, 'tis less Crime to pick his Pocket than another Mans; and if the World is free to buy a *Courant* full of Emptiness every Day, the Author is the more to be excused, and so far sure we may hope to be read as well as he.

But this is certain, that neither he nor his 20 Booksellers can have any thing to say, why they should thus impose upon us, but that we are all Fools and *Bubbles*, *and fit to be imposed upon*.

The first Peice of Publick News we shall begin with, is wholly Domestick, tho' it has a Title of Foreign. A Letter was sent to *Lloyd* the Coffee-man in *Lombard-street*, importing that the *French* had taken St. *Hellena*, and 15 Sail of *English East-India* Men there, and pretends to give us the Names of the Ships. Our

Our worthy Author of the *Review* has brought this Story before his Club, with his mythological Manner. But I must crave leave to tell him, he cannot obtain the Name of a Southsayer, for supposing this to be a Contrivance of the Stock-Jobbers, for a blind Man might ha' catch'd this Hare as well as he.

As to *Lloyd* the Coffee-man, we can by no means clear him, as he does, under the Title of Honest *Lloyd*; for as he has been us'd to tell all he knows in such Cases, and sometimes a little more; so if *Lloyd* had not been a Party to this Fraud, he ought to have known, as well as another, that those 15 *East-India* Men could no more meet at St. *Helena* all at a Time, than a *Mahometan*, a Coffee-man, and a Stock-Jobber could meet in Heaven together.

'Tis known if Mr. *Lloyd* be peculiar in any thing, 'tis in knowing the Time when Merchant Ships come in and go out, to and from all our Ports, and perhaps is good for little else, and he cannot be so ignorant, as not to know that those Ships went out at such wild and incoherent Distances of Time, as that in the Language of Trade it could not be.

The result of this Reflection is therefore thus, and we believe the Observation is very just. 1. That *Lloyd* the Coffee-man is a K——, and privy to the Cheat, a Party to the Fraud, and whether he had a Snack of the Gain or no, a great Share in the Villany:

Or 2. That he is a F——, and blew this Trumpet of Knavery, without giving himself leave to think, without examining his Lists, and rumaging his Memory for the time when the Ships went out.

As to the thing it self, and its being a Trick *of the Stock-Jobbers*, that is so easy to prove, and so exceeding plain, that the Author of the *Review* will have much ado to make good what he affirms, that his Paper shall never be charged with trifling, or proving what every Body knows, when he troubles his Club with examining whether it was a Stock-Jobbing Project or no.

The Author of these Sheets has the Misfortune to know so much of the Schemes and Plans of Stock-Jobbing Politicks, that he wonders this Trick should not be too gross to take, in this pretended clear sighted Age.

But for a full Demonstration of its being a meer Stock-Jobbing Forgery, he refers to the *Bubbles that were bit by it*, and that in a Fright sold their *East-India* Stock, desiring them to cast up their Accounts, and tell us how much Stock they sold upon this News, and who bought it.

If they are willing to expose their Folly so much, we can tell them that there was above 20000 *l.* Stock sold by Fools, and bought by K——s upon this Letter. And if the Enquirers please to apply themselves to a late piec'd up broken Broker, who took Sanctuary at Sir *T. C.* Country City House, and made a *White-Fryers* of the *Tower* of *London*, according to the Example of that worthy Candidate for the City Chair: we undertake that for a half *per Cent*, he shall give a List of their Names who bought this Stock; or if not, for half the Mony we will do it for them.

If any Man therefore enquires who writ the Letter to *L*—— the Coffee-man, let him come to us, we shall answer him by enquiring who bought 20000 *l. East India* Stock the next Day? to which Question, if Mr. —— the Broker does not answer, 'tis not his Ignorance but his Guilt that makes him silent.

But 'tis a strange thing to reflect, that the First Cheat being over, here comes a Letter which Mr. *Courant* is made the worthy Fool to publish; to *say off* the Substance of the former ——— and thus the Gamesters are playing the Cheat

[4]

back again, for there's as grand a Fraud in the Second Letter as was in the First.

The First Letter put the World upon parting with their Stock, and sunk the Value above 4 per Cent at once, now comes a Second Letter, and owning the fraud of the First, confesses it was a Villanous forgery to serve a turn, that is to sink the Stock; But now the end is answered, he writes to undeceive the World, that is in short, now the Stock is sunk and the Gang have laid out their Money, the Story must be unsaid again, that the Stocks may rise and they may sell off Hand at 4 per Cent profit, and so those who bought more Stock then they had Money to pay for, may sell it again in the same breath, and put the difference in their Pockets.

If this were not the Trick what need of sending a Letter to unsay the First; they wont pretend 'twas in justice to the Town to undeceive them, he that was Villain enough to form the first Cheat would never have troubled his head with the undeceiving the World had he not had a farther Cheat to drive by this Second Letter, every jot as wicked as the First.

To trace this Second Cheat, and so prove the Fact upon the very Persons, it needs only to examine whether those very Men who bought the Stocks the 3d and 4th of *August*, do not immediately part with the same Stock——on the first Rise in manner as above.

What a reproach is it to a Christian Nation that in the very Bowels of their Negotiation so scandalous, so open a practice of Cheating and Thieving is tollerated, or at least permitted by the Law---shall we pretend to Religion and Reformation of Manners, and suffer a debauchery in Trade, an infection in the morality of Buying and Selling: 'Tis a shame to the Protestant Religion, and to the whole Nations Morals—— the buying and selling of Pardons in the Popes Heaven jobbing Market is an Ass to this---all the Tricks and Cheats of *Bartholomew* Fair, or the Groom Porters are nothing to it---and it's as impossible for a meer Stock-jobber to be an honest Man as for a self-murtherer to be saved——to be a Stock-jobber and not morgage all the sence of Honour, Faith and Candor, is to be undone and come to nothing; no Rogue no Stock-jobber, the Man will be ruin'd, according to my Lord *Rochester*.

For Honesty's against all Common Sence,
Men must be Knaves, 'tis in their own defence.
If with known Cheats you I play upon the Square,
You I be Undone——
Nor will weak Fame your Reputation save,
The Knaves will all agree to call you Knave.
And all the subject matter of debate,
Is only who's a Knave of the first rate.

We hope our Reflections on this grand nusance of the Nation, are just; as to their being severe, we pretend to freedom of speech, and shall take that liberty with all sorts of People that we think they deserve without respect of *Persons, Powers* or *private revenge*. We scorn the malice of the Guilty, and defy the reproaches of that part of Mankind who Crush by their power the Tongues that speak the truth of them.

If News Writers *will lye* they shall hear of it; if Men will be wicked their Neighbours shall know it, our Reflections shall be proper and suitable, but, *stand clear Vice with both its Actors and Patrons*.

MDCCIV.

[5] Numb. 2.

THE
Master Mercury:

BEING

An ABSTRACT of the Publick NEWS:

With Plain and Impartial Reflections both on Persons and Things.

Thursday, August 8. 1704.

OUR last had the good Fortune to be so well received both as to the Design, as well as the Performance, that we should be unjust to our selves and the Publick, if we did not acknowledge it, and proceed to let them see how willing, as well as able, we are to please them.

We meet with some indeed who threaten us hard for falling so foul upon all the several kinds of Writers, as if we design'd to embroil our selves with the whole Party of Authors.

Indeed they are so numerous and so formidable, so clamorous and impertinent, that no Man who values his own Ease, will be concern'd with them.—— But who can forbear letting the Author of the *Review* know somebody knows something as well as himself.

Who can forbear telling the *Courant* that when he has nothing to say, he certainly comes out so often. —— *Facit Indignatio versum*, said *Juvenal* in the like Case. A Man can have no Fire in his Thoughts, if when his Pen is upon the Paper, he can forbear to let these Gentlemen know how the World sees themselves impos'd upon.

There are four Mails from abroad come in just as this is working off at the Press; but they come too late to incert any Part of them in this Paper; and therefore the Reader is desired to look on this, as a Paper of Yesterday, prepar'd before the News was come in.

But to leave these meaner Reflections we come to entertain the World with something we call News.

In our last Weeks Paper we have an Account from Admiral *Whetston* that a *Swedish* Man of War having under Convoy some Merchant Men refus'd to strike to the *English* Flag; whereupon the *Worcester* firing a Gun, the Commander sent his Boat on board to let our Admiral know his Orders were

B not

[6]

not to strike to any Nation whatever, or to that Effect: The *Worcester* upon this, taking no Notice of the Message, fir'd a Ball; upon which the *Swede* began the Fight, and poured in her Broadside upon the *Worcester*; the *Worcester* and the *Dover* engag'd her; she maintain'd the Fight with great Obstinacy, till being quite disabled, 100 of her Men kill'd, her Ancient or Ensign shot down, &c. she was taken, and all the Merchant-men who were under her Convoy.

We do not tell this Story as News, and hope no body will be so dull as to think so, the Town having had the Particulars above a Week ago; but as our principal Design is to make just Reflections, we think this Action deserves some Remark.

The first Question every body ask'd about this *Swedish* Captain, is whether he had really Orders for what he has done.

As to that, we are told his Commission and Instructions were brought up, and being laid before our Governors, it appear'd he had general Orders which justify him in the Action.

Without Question, if he had no Orders, he ought to be hang'd here, as well as at home; he ought to be hang'd here, as a Man that took upon him to quarrel with the *English* Nation on his own Account; and being no fair or declared Enemy, falls upon us, and destroys us all according to the best of his Power without Provocation, and therefore deserves no Quarter.

But he ought to be hang'd in *Sweden*, as a Man that has murdered 100 of his Master's Subjects, in throwing away their Lives on an Action which he had no Power or Right to do, and therefore is all one, as if he had sunk the Ship and drown'd them; for which he ought to be hang'd, and no doubt would have had his Due at his return. But if he had Orders for what he has done, then the Man has acted like a bold brave Fellow, and put his Master's Orders in Execution, with all the Gallantry and Valour suitable to the *Swedish* Nation, and like a Man of Honour,—— and thus our Observations will of course be remov'd from the Captain of the Ship to the King his Master.

And what then can the Meaning of this Action be? either it must be that the *Swede* pretends to be able to deal with the rest of *Europe* at Sea, or else that he designs particularly to affront her Majesty, and the whole *English* Nation, and seeks this for an occasion of Quarrel.

Indeed we cannot but observe that the Reputation of a certain Nation in the World has so sensibly decreased by the Knavery, Cowardice, and ill Conduct of her Commanders for some Years past, that some may cease to wonder they should receive Affronts, and be insulted at Sea, and perhaps the *Swedes* may think the *English* so too.

But 'tis well known the *English* Captains will fight, and so will their Seamen too; and we cannot but give a just Encomium to our Admiral, who when he perceived the audacious Boldness of this obstinate *Swede*, laid about him for the Honour of the *English* Nation, and the Dominion of the four Seas, and after a very obstinate Fight, took him Captive, with all his Men, Guns, &c.

Nor let any Man object the Disparity between one Ship and a whole Squadron; for we can tell him when some Commanders less brave and less daring than Admiral *Whetstone* has let the Enemy pass untought with, tho' the odds have been as great; nay, tho' the Riches of the Enemy would have tempted less Cowardly Captains than themselves,

selves; so much Men's Fear, will exceed their worst Vices, even Covetousness it self can't make a Coward fight.

I hope the Reader will accept it for a Caution that we are not to be supposed to mean any of the G———s, Rigb——, Lakes, Rakes, or R———s of our Nation, but some *Eutopian* Cowards that are unacquainted with *English* Valour.

To the immortal Honour and Glory of Admiral *Whetstone*, and his Squadron, they have made this known Experiment that the *English* Captains can fight, and particularly Capt. B——r in the *Worcester*, in spight of all the Reproaches of *Willmot*'s Executors, has let us know he can fight as well as ——— especially when he has not too much of another Man's Money on board.

As to a certain King, and his endeavouring to pick a Quarrel with the *English*, it seems plain to us he does his utmost that way, and indeed we cannot but think 'tis unkind in us to put his Majesty to so much Trouble in the Case, since he has tried so many ways to provoke us before, as makes us pass in the World for a Nation of vast Moderation. ———

This Moderation is a very ambiguous Phrase, and perhaps we may have Occasion to make frequent use of it in these Papers; particularly we cannot avoid saying, that when a Nation is immoderately affronted, they seem to be very moderately wise that cannot see it, and to have very moderate Courage that dare not resent it.

We are not going about to reflect upon the Wisdom of our Superiors in the matter, as if they did not know when it was fit for them to make Peace or War,—but we cannot but reflect upon that Nation, or Prince, let it be who it will, that thinks we may have any thing put upon us, yon Presumption that our present Circumstances will not suffer us to resent it.

When a single Ship has been thus sent to affront a whole Nation, it has always been taken as a seeking Occasion to quarrel; so when King *Charles* the Second wanted something to make the Foundation of a Quarrel with the *Dutch*, the *Henrietta* Yacht was ordered to Sea, with Instruction, when she met with the *Dutch* Fleet, she should fire a Gun to cause them all to strike to the *English* Colours; away goes the Yacht, and meets the whole Fleet; she comes up with the Admiral and fires a Gun, which in the Language of the Sea is, *Don't you see who I am, and whose Colours I carry? don't you know your Duty to my Master's Flag? why don't you pull off your Hat to my Master?* The *Dutch* Admiral who saw the meaning of it, refus'd the Compliment, but did not offer to fire at the Yacht; the Yacht next fires a Gun with a Shot, which in the Sea Phrase, is as much as to say, you *Dutch* Dogs, *if you don't strike immediately, I am a coming*: when this would not do, and yet he could not provoke the *Dutch* to fire again, they carefully avoiding giving any Occasion or Pretence of a Quarrel, up comes the *little haughty Cockboat* and pours in her Broad-side of four Guns, I suppose, or thereabouts, into the *Dutch* Admiral of 96 Guns; all this could not provoke the wary Admiral; and so the Yacht went strutting thro' the whole Fleet, and came home again without his Errand.

It was reported, how true we will not determine, that the *Dutch* Admiral caused ten Men on board every Ship, as the Yacht passed by, to stand upon the Fore-castle of their Ships, and letting down their Breeches, shew'd the *English-man* their Backsides as he passed by and then halloo'd him along, and let him go.

Thus the Design was lost, and the Pretence of a War could not be found; but as the Government then had resolved on a War, they began it at last without a Pretence. *Smirna Fleet for that.*

If this Action of the *Swedish* Man of War be done on a like Account, if he was sent to seek an Occasion of a War, our Opinion, with Submission to our Superiors, is, in short, thus.

1. If 'tis meant to provoke us to begin a War, the *Swede* is defeated; for as the Action is an Affront to the *English* Nation, we have sufficiently revenged that Affront in taking the Ship, and the Tables are turned; the *Swedes* may reclaim their Ship, and see if it will be delivered again.

2. If the *Swede* wants an Occasion to declare against the *English*, he has it; he may demand the Ships, and declare War upon the Refusal.

And certainly the Prudence of the *Swede* is but very little seen in it; if the *English* had a Mind to have quarrelled with the *Swedes*, they had Occasion enough before, and have none the more now; if the *Swedes* have a Mind to quarrel with the *English*, they may do it without any Pretence, and have none the more for this Action.

If our Paper had room for this time, it should with our Merchants Joy for the Arrival of the *Virginia* Fleet, which as our Accounts say, are arrived safe to the Number of 130 Sail under the Convoy of 2 Men of War, that is to say, 2 Men of War appointed by the Government; and God Almighty knowing, as well as we, they should have need of them, sent them 2 more which coming home from the *West Indies*, joyn'd them 2 days after they came out.

Our Government sure is the best in the World; what Pen is sufficient to give them their due Praises! The Admiralty of *England*, like the Heavenly Influences, extends to every Part of the mighty body of Trade, under its Conduct and Government: not an Angle of our Navigation but the Ships of War are directed to search for Ships, and Merchants, in Order to afford them their Convoy and Protection.

Is there 150 Sail of Ships bound home with Tobacco from the Capes of *Virginia*, whose Cargo is of vast Moment to this Nation, and pays 150000 *l*. Custom to the Crown; such a Concern merits a proportioned Care, and the Diligence is very remarkable; no less than 2 large Men of War, carrying together almost 100 Pieces of Cannon are sent to bring them off; and to let the Enemy see that 'tis in vain for them to pretend to attack our Fleet so carefully guarded, and so powerfully defended by our Ships of War.

But as this is a Subject too large to be finish'd in the Conclusion of this Paper, we refer it to the next.

MDCCIV.

Number 3 is lacking.

[13]   Numb. 4.

THE
Master Mercury:

BEING

An ACCOUNT of the Great Battle of *HOCHSTETTEN*;

With the *French* King's Letter to the Arch-Bishop of *Paris*, to Sing *TE DEUM*.

Thursday, August 17. 1704.

ALL our Accounts are full of the extraordinary Particulars of the Victory obtained at *Hochstetten*: All the Accounts being put together, and compar'd, we think the Abstract of the Battel is as follows,

That the *French* having formed the Design of falling upon Prince *Eugene* of *Savoy*, as he lay near *Donawert*, seperated from the Duke of *Marlborough*, march'd with exceeding Secrecy and Swiftness round by the Bridge at *Lawinghen*, with their whole Army; but that the Duke of *Marlbrough* having Intelligence of the said March, first sent Lieutenant General *Lumley* with 20 Battalions to reinforce Prince *Eugene* for Fear of a Surprize, and followed with the whole Army the next Day; that being joyn'd they advanc'd with a Design to possess the Camp at *Hochstetten*, near the *Danube*, but that at they found the *French* had got thither before them; that thereupon they resolved to attack them; to which end, they march'd the 13th early, and appeared before the Camp of the *French* by 7 in the Morning; that they Cannonaded each other from nine to one, during which time the Confederate Army were employed in laying their Bridges over a Rivulet which was in the Front for their Foot to pass, and their Horse wheeling to form their Line; that about one, the whole Army mov'd in one Line to attack the *French*, who were drawn up in two entire Armies; the Mareschal *de Tallard* commanded the Right with the Forces lately come from the *Rhine*, among which were the Horse of the Houshold of *France*, and the Flower of the *French* Troops, in Number about 6000; the Elector of *Bavaria*, and the Mareschal *Marsin* com-

D   manded

manded the Left, and had with him the *Bavarian* Cavalry, among which were 3000 Cuirasseers, his whole Body being about 32000 Men.

The Confederate Army were drawn up in the same manner in two distinct Armies; each had their Wings of Horse, with the Foot in the Center, and each had great Bodies of Reserve both of Horse and Foot; Prince *Eugene* of *Savoy*, with the Imperial and *Prussian* Troops, with the Prince of *Hannover*, and the Imperial Generals, commanded the Right, and were together about 26000 The Left was formed by the *English* and *Dutch* Troops, including the *Hessian*, *Danish*, and *Wirtemberg* Troops in *English* Pay, and were led by the Duke of *Marlborough*, the Prince of *Hesse Cassell*, the Lord *Cutts*, and the rest of the *English* and *Dutch* Generals, and made up about 28000 Men.

The Duke of *Bavaria* began the Fight, and charged the Right of the Confederate Army, led by Prince *Eugene* of *Savoy*, with such irresistible Fury, that tho' the Imperial Horse received them with all the Steadiness imaginable, yet the *Bavarian* Cuirasseers charged thro' the Line, and disorder'd some Regiments, pushing them near a 100 Paces, but this not without a most obstinate Fight, and Great Slaughter on both sides.

The Duke of *Marlborough*, to support this Wing which he found so hard press'd, form'd a Second Line in with the Troops of Reserve, and some Horse which he led to their Relief, repuls'd the *Bavarians*, and restor'd the Battel.

During this Action, the *English* and *Dutch* Horse in the left Wing of the Confederate Army, Charg'd the *French* right Wing with extraordinary Gallantry, and with doubtful success; the Troops of the *Horshold* behaving themselves with their usual bravery; the Infantry led on by the Lord *Cutts*, Charg'd the main of Monsieur *Tallards* Body, and were received with great Resolution, and thus the whole Armies were Engag'd with inexpressible Violence on every side; when the Duke of *Marlborough* finding all parts in a very good Condition, at the head of a great Body of Infantry, broke into the Centre, parted the two Armies; and falling with a Fury not to be resisted on the Horse of Marshal *Tallards* Left, put them into Confusion, and pushed them to the Rear of their infantry; who thus abandoned by their Horse, were soon disorder'd, and then follow'd a terrible Slaughter, the Horse were pushed to that Extremity, that 30 Squadrons took the *Danube* in the utmost Confusion, where very few of them escap'd.

All the Infantry that could make any Retreat rallyed in a Village which was in the Rear, where, tho' they were surrounded by the *English* Army, and Charg'd on every side, they made a desperate Defence, till seeing the Cannon brought against them, they threw down their Arms and yielded at discretion; these amounted to 27 entire Battallions and 12 Squadrons of Dragoons.

The Right of the *French* being thus wholly defeated, the *Confederates* under Prince *Eugene* fought with the more Vigor, and the Duke of *Bavaria* retreated, most of his Foot being entirely Ruined, except about 12 Battalions, and 20 Squadrons of his Horse stood firm, the whole Field being clear of the rest; but these being Charg'd afresh were broke and disorder'd, and not above 25 Squadrons went off with the Duke of *Bavaria*, who passing the *Danube* at *Lavingen*, is said to have fled towards *Augsburgh*.

Thus ended the Bloodiest Battel, and thus was gained the greatest Victory this Age has ever seen, the Fight lasted from 1 to near 8 at Night.

The Enemy's Camp was entirely taken, with all their Tents, Baggage, Carriages, Ammunition, 90 pieces of Cannon,

non, and 122 Colours and Standards, the rest of the Booty which fell to the share of the Soldiers is incredible.

They have 15000 Prisoners, among which is the Marshal *Tallard*, and Sixteen other Generals, 1500 Officers, besides 3000 Horses, and above 30000 small Arms.

The REFLECTOR.

As this is the greatest overthrow that ever the *French* met with for above 200 Years past, so we cannot find in any of our Histories an Action like it. The Great and Bloody Battel of *Leipsick*, between the brave *Gustavus Adolphus*, and old General *Tilly*, comes the nearst to it, in which the Imperial Army being 44000 Men, was Routed and entirely Beaten, after a most Dreadful and Obstinate Fight. There was 8000 Foot at the end of the Battle retreated to a Village as the *French* did here, but with this difference, that as the *French* here laid down their Arms, the other fought to the last, would never accept of Quarter, though they knew their General was fled, but were cut in pieces Rank and File as they were drawn up, and never turned their Backs.

Now as the World is full of Joy, and Expresses come from every part with News, our Reflectors pretend to tell you by way of Advice from *Paris*, That this News having been brought to his most Chrstian Majesty, after some serious consideration of the Circumstances, and remembring that he ought to put the best Face on it for the use of his Subjects, he is said to send the following Letter to the Arch-Bishop of *Paris*, in Order to sing *Lachrima* in the Church of *Nostre Dame* at *Paris*.

The *French* King's Letter to the Arch-Bishop of *Paris*.

COUSIN,

OUR Cousin the Duke of Bavaria having earnestly solicited us to send him a Powerful Assistance of our Troops, in Order to the driving away of the Enemy's Army out of his Territories, and the preserving him in his Fidelity and Adherence to us and our Cause; We thought fit to Order our Cousin the Marshal Count de Tallard, General of our Army's, to march from the Upper Rhine *with so many Troops, as with the usual blessing of God, and the success of our Arms, might be sufficient to prevent all the Designs of the Enemy, and effectually to Succour his Highness*; which having been performed by our said Cousin the Marshal de Tallard, *notwithstanding all the pretended Opposition of Prince* Eugene *of Savoy, who contented himself to be the Spectator of the March of our Troops, without concerning himself to try their known Valour and Resolution.*

And whereas after the Conjunction of our said Troops, the Enemy thought fit forthwith to abandon all their Conquests in Bavaria, *and to leave his Highness, our Ally the Duke of* Bavaria *in full possession of his own Country.*

And that being Persued by our Troops over the Danube, *a Great and Bloody Battle has hapned, in which the Valour and Intrepidity of our Troops, has according to their constant Custom appear'd, particularly in that, being overpower'd with the Numbers, 30 Squadrons of our Houshold chose rather to perish in the* Danube, *than to accept of Quarter from the Enemy; and the rest of our said Army with our Cousin the Marshal de* Tallard, *and 27 Battalions of our Foot, and 12 Squadrons of our Dragoons, with most of our General Officers, after a great Slaughter of the Enemy, and a most admirable and incredible Resistance, have committed themselves to the Enemy as Prisoners of War, thereby reserving Themselves and their Valour for our further Service, and for the Revenging the Quarrel of this day.*

I can therefore no longer delay rendring my thanks to Almighty God, for his continued Blessing on the Success of my Arms, and particularly for the safety of my Cousin the Marshal de Tallard, *and the rest of our Army, and for that our Cousin the Duke of* Bavaria *has also Retreated with some of his Troops out of the Battle, and for the great Slaughter of the Enemy upon this Occasion — Wherefore our pleasure is, that you Cause* Te Deum *to be Sung as is usual on the like occasion, in the Cathedral Church of our good City of* Paris, &c.

Given at Verfailles, *August* 14. 1704.

We are inform'd by the disposition of the Country, as well as by the report of those who came from thence, that the Reduction of the Duke of *Bavaria*, seems now so very certain, that Prince *Eugene* of *Savoy* is already march'd for *Italy* with 16000 Men, to joyn Count *Leiningen*, who lies with 12000 *Germans* in the *Trentine*, and with that united Force to enter the *Milanese*, and relieve the Duke of *Savoy*.

If this be Confirmed, *and the Nature of the thing seems to imply as much*, the Duke *de Vendosme* may chance to have but an ill time of it in *Italy*; and if the least Disaster should befall him there, that Army may come as short home as Monsieur *Tallard*.

The *French* Power has receiv'd such a blow by this Defeat in *Bavaria*, that it is not possible for any Body to guess at the Consequence.

We are sometimes apt to think that the Duke *de Vendosme* will have Orders to abandon *Italy*, and force his Way thro' *Piemont*, while his Troops are whole, and then face about upon the Duke of *Savoy*, and act upon the Defensive there.

This is conjectur'd, only because it seems rational to believe, that the King of *France* may recall some Troops from that side to prevent the ill Consequence of this Battle, and provide for the Confederates on the *Rhine*; for if the *Bavarians* should hold out, 'tis thought the *French* will not venture any more Succours so far from home; and if not, the Imperial Army under Prince *Lewis* of *Baden*, though not above 25000, will be sufficient to reduce the Duke of *Bavaria*, and the Duke of *Marlborough* may show the *French* the Victorious *English* Banners, upon the Banks of the *Rhine*, before this Campaign is over.

But tho we care not to insult the Duke of *Bavaria* in his Affliction; yet we cannot but ask the World this Question, who he must blame if the Emperor should refuse him any Conditions? And all Men may see the Consequence of unreasonable Ambition in this Prince, who aiming to be *aut Cæsar aut Nullus*, is in a fair way to be the last for endeavouring to be the first.

Our Next will entertain the World with one of the greatest Wonders of this Age; a fortified Town taken by our Sailors; wooden Walls and stone Walls fighting for the Victory at *Gibralter*, and wooden Walls carried it: From whence we shall pretend to tell the World, our Fleet are able to do great things, *if, &c.*

MDCCIV.

Numb. 5.

THE Master Mercury:

BEING

An ABSTRACT of the Publick NEWS:

With the REFLECTOR.

Monday, August 21. 1704.

WE cannot think it to the purpose to repeat the several Accounts of the Victory obtained in *Bavaria*, and therefore refer our Reader for the Particulars of that Action to our last, only with this Addition, that the particular Names of the Regiments, which were oblig'd to surrender at Discretion, are as follows.

	Squad.		Squad.
Dragoons of the Queen	2.	*Vasse*	3.
Marshal de Camp Gen	3.	*Rockan*	4.

In all 12 Squadrons.

Infantry.	Battal.	Infantry.	Battal.
Navarre	3.	*Monfort*	2.
Languedock	3.	*Senetterre*	2.
Sarlauben	2.	*Aunix*	2.
St. Sogene	2.	*Greber Alemand*	2.
Blois	1.	*Provence*	1.
Blevier	2.	*Merarcaux*	1.
La Ferr	2.	*Artois*	2.
Bolonois	1.		

In all 27 Battalions.

The next strange and wonderful Piece of Intelligence is from our Fleet, as follows.

Sir *Cloudsley Shovel* had received Orders from *Lisbon*, to sail and joyn the Fleet commanded by Sir *George Rook*, who not being able to fight the *French* Fleet, nor to take *Barcellona*, as was expected, was sailed out of the *Straits*, and came into *Lagos* Bay to *Water*.

Accordingly Sir *Cloudsley Shovel* joyned them; and they immediately sailed into the *Straits*; and being on the *Africk* about 7 Leagues East from *Tetuan*, they called a Council of War, and resolved to attack the Town of *Gibralter* in *Spain*.

Persuant to this Resolution, they sailed into the Bay of *Gibralter* the 21st, and immediately the Prince of *Hesse* landed with 1800 Marines, and posted himself on the Isthmus, which joyns the Town to the Main, at the same time cutting off all Communication between the Town and

and Country, and preventing the Inhabitants either removing their Effects, or making their Escape.

This done, two small Squadrons were directed to place themselves on either side the Mole, so as with most Convenience to batter the Place.

The Town was then summoned, but the Governour answer'd *a la Spagnole*; all things being prepared for reducing him to more Reason, the Ships begin to fire the 23d in the Morning early, and they plyed both the Town and the *Mole-head* so warmly, that they threw above 15000 Shot in less than 6 Hours time.

By the fury of this Fire the Enemy were beaten from their Works, and most of their Guns dismounted, and the Admiral took that opportunity to assault the the Fort at the *South mole head*, and all the Boats were order'd to be man'd for the said Attack; the Boats Commanded by Captain *Whitaker* made all the Expedition possible, but when they came to the Fort, they found the Platform already in the possession of the *English*; Captain *Hicks* and Captain *Jumper*, whose Ships lay nearest, having landed their Men before the rest could come up, and carried the Work by Storm, notwithstanding the *Spaniards* had blown up the Fortification on the *Mole*, and with it 40 of our Men, with 2 Lieutenants, and wounding 60 others; Captain *Whitaker*'s Men finding this work done to their Hands advanc'd towards the Town, and took a Redoubt that was built in the mid-way between the *Mole* and the Town, by which they became Masters of the Enemies Cannon, which they prepared to turn upon the Town.

All things being in this posture, a Peremptory Message was sent to the Governour to surrender or to expect no Quarter, upon which the Governour who had better considered of it Capitulated the 24th in the Morning, and the Prince of *Hesse* took possession of the Out-works the same day: the Articles are in short as follows.

1st. *That the Garrison, as well Officers as Souldiers, shall march out with their Arms, Baggage, Colours, &c. and the Officers and Inhabitants with their Horses, 3 Peices of Brass Cannon, 12 Charges of Powder and Ball, and shall take with them Provisions of Bread, Wine and Flesh for Six Days.*

2d. *That they march out in 3 Days, their Baggage shall not be search'd, what they cannot carry with them may remain to be sent for, and they shall have what Carts and Boats they have occasion for.*

3d. *All that will stay, as well Inhabitants as Souldiers and Officers of the Town, shall enjoy the same Priviledges as in King Charles the II. time, their Religion and Tribunals remain untouch'd, taking an Oath of Fidelity to King Charles the III.*

4th. *All Magazines to be discovreed and delivered up, all Subjects of the* French, *to be excepted out of the Capitulation, their Effects to be Seized and their Persons Prisoners of War.*

Thus the Town was surrender'd with a 100 Guns and all necessary Ammunition, the Prince of *Hesse* took Possession in the Name of *King Charles the* III. whom he caus'd immediatly to be proclaim'd, and the Admiral leaving a Garrison of 800 Marines in the Place, Sailed for the Coast of *Africk* as some say to Attack *Ceuta*.

On Saturday Night and since the writing of this Paper, we had two Mails from *Holland*, by which we are inform'd that the Victory at *Hochstet* begins to show it self in its happy Consequences.

The Elector of *Bavaria* has abandoned his Country to the Mercy of the Confederates, and collecting all his Garrisons to form an Army, has retreated with them towards *Ulm*, with intent, as it is believed, to joyn the Duke *de Villeroy*, whereupon *Augsburg*, *Munich*, and several other Places have sent to desire the Protection of the *English* Army. The Trenches before *Ingolstat* were opened the 15th; and *Bavaria* is very likely to be en-

entirely in the Hands of the Confederates.

From *Poland*, we are told there has been a bloody Battel between the *Swedes* and the *Lithuanians*; in which, the latter are worsted with the Loss of 3000 Men, 28 Pieces of Cannon, and 40 Standards; and that they hourly expect News of another Battel between Kings of *Sweden* and *Poland*.

We also hear the Duke of *Bavaria* would have capitulated with the Confederates on the same Condition formerly proposed to him, but it was rejected.

The REFLECTOR.

As the sacred Story tells of the *Israelites* after *Saul* had behaved himself like a Man in the Cause of his Country, so we may say of Sir *G. R.* Where are the Men that said this Man should not Command the *English* Fleet?

Who dare say Sir *G. R.* won't fight? bring out your *Observator*, your *Reviews*, &c. and let them be slain for Disturbers of the Peace, Fomenters of Jealousies and Discontents among her Majesties Subjects, and for Slanderers and Calumniators of our Admirals and Sea Commanders.

'Tis not for us to stand on shore and tell an Admiral when to fight and when to save the Queens Ships, we can never judge of Winds or Tides, we cannot tell how fast the *French* Ships can Sail, how much some Ships can out sail others, especially when one sort are willing to get away and the others have no Mind to overtake them; to Judge and Condemn Folks therefore at a distance cannot be fair.

You see Gentlemen what our Admirals can do for the Publick Service, when they finds it convenient to Act, and to exert their Power; we cannot therefore but Condemn these People very much who show their ill Nature by reflecting on them, as if they might have done the same thing at *Cadiz* and at *Barcellona*.

The mistake is very obvious, it was thought fit rather to Land at Port St. *Maries*, where there was good Booty to be had, then boldly at once to venture upon the Town it self and knock our heads against Stone Walls, and we appeal to Sir *Henry B-----fis* whether the Enemy was not beaten there much to our advantage; impoverishing an Enemy is beating them, and they that cannot see into the vast advantage of that Expedition, we advise them to Dr----to cure their Eye-sight.

Why look ye, Gentlemen, first of all here was a rich Trading Port taken full of Wealth and Merchandizes, this we plunder'd as heartily as ever *Tartar* Ravag'd a Village in *Hungary*, there was Cubbards full of Plate, Cabinets full of China, Ware-houses full of Silks, Cellers full of Wine, Cloysters full of Nuns, and which was still most agreeable to us all, no Souldiers, no fighting.

What if we did give the Writer of the *Gazette* a hint to tell the World the firing of Guns, the Noise and the flashes at our coming off, resembled the day of Judgment (-------*Gazette*, Num. -------) for all some People are so angry with him on that Head, the Man was in the right so far as any body can guess of that Day, for as we all believe there will be no Cannon or Bombs fired at that time, so the Devil a Gun was fired at us when we came off, but what we fired our selves for Joy we were got away.

'Tis without question that we touch'd the *Spaniards* in a most sensible part, we gave them a tast of *English* Courage, we let them know we were as able to fight against 100 Butts of Sherry as against 100 great Guns upon the Puntals and Forts with Damned hard Names, as well as hard Walls at *Cadiz*. You

[20]

You may easily guess how we manag'd them, since in the little time we possest that place, as we are told the *Spaniards* own, we did them Damage amounting to 2532000 Dollars, and some *Spaniards* ask our Regiment, taken Prisoners of War in *Portugal*, if the *English-men* are Christians, meaning as we suppose, that fighting with such extraordinary Fury at Port *St. Mary*, they thought they were Devils not Men.

Wherefore this Action at Port St. *Mary's*, having in our opinion had such extraordinary Effects on the *Spaniards*, filled them with such Terror at the *English* Name, and so much prepar'd them to revolt and come over to their new King, we cannot but let the World see as far as we are able, how Sr. *G. Rook* has been injur'd and traduc't by People who know no better, and the whole Navy asperst, as if they got more Mony than Honour by that Voyage.

Without doubt the Generals knew what they did when they committed that Town to Discretion, and what a great weakning it would be to the Enemy to ruin their Merchants, to knock out the Heads of their Buts of Wine, and let it run Knee-deep into the Cellars, to break a-pieces their fine Sashes and Glass Cabinets, and destroy all they could not bring away with them, and the like; and as for those that asperse our People, and say they acted against Orders, all the World that understand any thing of War must laugh at so malicious, as well as empty a Reflection, since they cannot suppose such a thing, because the Officers were not immediately hanged upon so manifest a Breach of their Instructions, and there is no Question but those Gentlemen entrusted in that Expedition both with the Army, Navy, and Honour of *England*, would effectually have taken Care to have had their Orders punctually executed, and not have failed severely to punish the Trespass.

Let no Man therefore any more reflect on that Action, or call it a Miscarriage; can it be a Miscarriage to invade an Enemy, to insult one of their Capital Ports, to land in Sight of the strongest Fortresses in the Kingdom, to plunder one of their richest Towns, do them two Millions of Spoil, and come off again without any Loss.

This sort of People are never pleased but with bloody Noses; like our People that go to see the Prize-Fighters, if they don't cut one another, and they don't see the Blood run about, they cry it's a Cheat, and they fight booty; so if our Admiral had attack'd *Cadiz* hand over head, lost 2 or 3 thousand of the Queen's best Soldiers, and 10 or 12 of her best Ships, all had been well, and he had done like a Man of Honour, as well as a Man of War.——But when he acted like a true *English* Admiral, took Care to do the Enemy a great deal of Damage, and to go where most Money was to be got, and least Blood to be shed, took Care to save the Queen's Soldiers and the Queen's Ships, then he must be traduc'd and affronted by every Scribler, and Mr. *Observator* don't like him, because he don't furnish his Country-man with fighting Stories.

We think we cannot do our Country better service, than in clearing up this Gentleman's Character to the World, undeceiving the People in refference to our Naval Affairs, and therefore in Spight of Mr. *Observator*, or his Countryman, we shall in the process of these Papers, endeavour to let the World see how far the worthy Character of Her Majesty's Vice Admiral has been ill treated and abused.

MDCCIV.

Numbers 6-10 are lacking.

[41]   Numb. 1.

THE
Master Mercury:

BEING

An ABSTRACT of the Publick NEWS:

With the REFLECTOR.

Monday, September 11. 1704.

THE Barrenness of the Town for News, occasion'd by the want of 3 Forreign Posts, puts all our News-Writers to a great loss for something to fill up their Papers, that their Readers may have something for their Money.

It cannot but be a little diverting to the Town, to see themselves plaid with by our News-Writers; how one day Mr. *Courant* gives us a List of our Fleet, then of the *French* Fleet, and how far asunder the Names stand to help fill up the Paper; 'tis odd to see our selves fiddl'd out of our Money, then there comes a long Letter from Monsieur *Puiseux* to the *Swiss* Cantons, the first part fills up a whole Paper, the remainder is to help for another, and so on.

Mr. *London Post*, he goes on with a great deal of good Nature to reform us all and bring us to our Senses, *by running out of his own. That incorrigible Scribler* makes such Blunders as no Man ever made but himself, and such as must make us still suspect that he has some Plot in it, for tis morally impossible he shou'd be such an eternal Dunce, unless he was possest with a Spirit of Nonsense to excel all his Neighbours.

Thus, in one of his Papers he tells us *P. L.* of *Baden* has open'd the *Frontiers* before *Ingolstadt*, in another, that the

L *Saxons*

Saxons are moving towards the Frontiers of the Cardinal *Primate*; above all, he is a rare Man at Latin, which may be seen in a Quotation of his about St. *Peter*, in his Paper of *August* 30. which we defie all the Town to make *English* of.

As we have no Forreign Post, we shall not pretend to Forreign News, and therefore shall examine the Town for News.

It has been a very sickly Time, and Gripings and Convulsions have carried above 230 People in a Week, some of our Bills have amounted to above six hundred in a Week, which, considering that 'tis a time when vast numbers of People are out of Town, the *Court*, the *Parliament*, *Term*, *Army* and *Fleet* all abroad, is a greater number than as we believe has died in a Week at any time since the Plague Year. The Learned ascribe the great Cause to the Heats and drought we have had for above three Months past, and withal to the great plenty of Fruit of all sorts.

On the day before the Thanksgiving the Lord Mayor, Aldermen, and Common Council went up with a large Train of Coaches to St. *James*'s, to present the City Address, and to Congratulate Her Majesty on the late glorious Victory.

The Queen receiv'd them like her self, with abundance of Goodness, Knighted Mr. *Woolf*, one of the Sheriffs, and gave them all the usual Demonstrations of Her Majesties Favour.

The Address being extraordinary, and as we suppose is to be follow'd by all the Cities and Corporations in *England*, we thought fit to give a Copy, as follows.

To the QUEEN's Most Excellent Majesty.

The humble Address of the Lord Mayor, Aldermen and Commons of Your City of *London*, in Common Council Assembled.

Dread Sovereign!

ALthough from a Mature and Impartial *Consideration* of your great *Wisdom* steddy *Resolution* and indefatigable *Care*, our Hopes were raised to a very high Pitch; yet we did not dare to equal them to those great and glorious Successes with which the Almighty hath blessed the just and necessary Arms of Your Majesty and your Allies.

The Banks of the *Danube* shall Eccho *Marlborough* to all future Ages! The Duke, who by his Courage and Conduct, hath at one hearty Push settled the tottering Empire, relieved Savoy, chastised the Elector of Bavaria, and curbed the Ambition of the French King: But it is (under God) to Your Majesty's great Judgment (demonstrated in your wise Choice of such a General) that these great things are owing.

Such Eminent Mercies do at once raise all our united Hearts into one Sacrifice of Praise and Thanksgiving to our Great and Gracious God, and turn our Eyes on you, Madam, his Vicegerent, whose sincere Piety and constant Devotion are the only Title we can pretend to such signal Blessings.

May the same good Providence shower down all Blessings upon your Sacred Person, and make you the Glorious Instrument of settling Europe in a secure and a lasting Peace: May Your Majesty long live, the Terror of your Enemies, the Defence of your injured Neighbours, and the Delight of your Subjects; And may you, without the least Interruption, Enjoy all the Pleasure and Satisfaction that a Queen can have, who Reigns absolutely in the Hearts of an Obedient and a Grateful People.

[43]

On *Thursday* last was our Day of Thanksgiving for the Glorious Victory over the *French* and *Bavarians* at *Hochstet*. The Queen came in great State, and with the usual Solemnity to St. *Paul*'s Cathedral, where great Preparations had been made for Her Majesties Reception; several new Anthems made on purpose, and all the best Musick that could be had.

The Appearance of the Nobility and Gentry was very great, the Season of the Year considered, three Regiments of the City Trained Bands lined the Streets from the Church to *Temple Bar*, and two Regiments of *Westminster* Militia did the like to St. *James*'s, a Body of the Foot Guards took Post within the Walls of the Church, and the Duke of *Ormond*'s Troop of Horse Guards follow'd the Queen's Coach.

The share the City had in the Show, besides the three Regiments of the Trained Bands, was as follows.

All the Companies in their Gowns and their Formalities, stood in Galleries built on purpose on both sides the Street from St. *Dunstan*'s Church to the Church Door, with their Musick Playing at the head of every Gallary.

My Lord Mayor and Court of Aldermen, with the two Sheriffs, all on Horse-back, Rid before the Queen's Coach, the Lord Mayor carrying the Sword bare headed before the Queen. There was another Gentleman who expected to make his Figure in Scarlet, and came for that purpose to the Hall, but some Objections happening, he was pleas'd to order his fine Horse to be sent homeward, afterwards refus'd to Grace the Queen with his Company.

There was some small Disasters happen'd, as is usual in such great Crowds. A *French* Barbre in *Devereux Court* near the *Temple*, being upon the Duty in the Trained Bands, was taken with some suddain Fit and fell down dead.

A Shed among the Works at St. *Paul*'s, being loaded with People fell down, and several People were hurt, but none kill'd.

After the Show was over there happen'd some Dispute between the White Regiment of the City Militia and the Foot Guards, who met in the narrow part of *Fleet-street*, some high words past between the Officers, and 'twas fear'd it might have come to Blows, but the Trained Bands at last march'd away thro' *Chancery-lane* to avoid yielding the way.

The Day concluded with Feasting within Doors, Firing of Guns, Bonefires, and Illuminations without, here and there a little Drunkenness came in as the *addenda* to the Joy, and so the Day went over.

The REFLECTOR.

THere is nothing so impertinent in this World as City Ceremonies, such a Day our Aldermen must ware Scarlet, another Day Crimson, sometimes they go on Foot, sometimes by Water, sometimes they'll Ride in Coaches, sometimes on Horseback, and so contrary is the Methods of their Cavalcads, that they'll go in Coaches to St. *James*'s, or to *Hampton Court*, and Ride a Horseback to Church. But that which is oddest of all, and which seems to have something very ill natur'd, is that when an honest Gentleman had been at the trouble to borrow some fine Clothes both for himself and his Horse, and to show his extraordinary Respect to Her Majesty, had put himself into an Alderman's Figure, our ill natur'd upper House Peers of the Gold Chain Men of Scarlet and fine Trappings, would not let him Ride with them.

The

(44)

The Observation we make from thence is this, that since they are so incoherent in their Solemnities, they need not have been so Nice with a certain Gentleman, tho' he had a mind to have rid in their Livery, and in our opinion it would not have been so Incongruous as some Gentlemen thought: for why not a Scarlet Lawyer as well as a Scarlet Alderman: Besides L. M. who was so much concern'd with *Jefferies* in all his Proceedings, might have some greater Pretence to the Bloody Colour, as having been a Favourite in the reign of a Scarlet Chancellor.

This is a strange Age, that Men of Place and Worship should be so rude; what harm had it been to have let a Man of no Merit have rid among them; if no body should Ride there but Men of Merit, it might be very troublesome to the City in their future Elections; besides this Gentlemans admittance could have done no harm to the Constitution, since he that never signify'd any thing any where else, could not signifie much there.

'Twas hard there should be so much discontent on all sides, there ought to have been no complaining on any occasion, no body should have been made Chagrin in a day of such General Joy.

Some ill-natur'd People reflect upon the Citys waiting on the Queen without a Mouth with them; that they carry'd an Address up, and when they came there had no body speak to it, and were fain to Imploy one of their Common Officers to read it.

These are People that only watch for somthing to Cavil at, since 'tis plain they had a Gentleman of undoubted Reputation as to his Parts, Learning and Eloquence, who the City to their great Honour, as well as his, thought fit to make their Orator for the Day.

Let no Man therefore doubt any more of the business being done to the honour of the City and Her Majesty's satisfaction. If any enquiring Person shall have sense little enough to Cavil at the matter, 'tis a sufficient answer to tell them, it was perform'd in the absence of the Recorder, by that worthy Gentleman and great Lawyer, the Honourable Common-Serjeant of the City.

This is Answer enough, this is the Man the City thought fit to honour with the Office of that day; or, rather this is the Man did the City the honour to speak for them: How should Her Majesty but be pleas'd? How could she but receive an Address very Graciously, presented to her by the City of *London*, and read to Her by so Excellent an Orator.

The Noble Speech he made to Her Majesty on the occasion, may be a sufficient Answer to all these Cavils, at which Her Majesty was so extreamly well pleas'd, that She immediately Knighted Sr. *Joseph Woolf*, one of the Sheriffs of the City, and was resolv'd to come and hear some more City Musick the next Day.

The Knighting of the Sheriff had been matter of City Speculation for a long time, and some thought it had been a Tryal of Skill in the City, among some Folks of Power, but the Queen who was no Party to the sides, Dubb'd the Gentleman to the exceeding Mortification of some that valued themselves upon the Negative, but of this in another opportunity.

ADVERTISEMENT.

A True State of the Difference between Sir Geo. Rook, Knt. and Will. Colepeper, Esq; Together with an Account of the Tryal of Mr. Nathanael Denew, Mr. Robert Britton, and Mr. John Merriam, before the Right Honourable Sir John Holt, Knt. Lord Chief Justice of England, on an Indictment for the Designs and Attempts therein mentioned against the Life of the said William Colepeper on Behalf of the said Sir George Rook.

MDCCIV.

[41]   Numb. 12

THE
Master Mercury:
BEING

An ABSTRACT of the Publick NEWS

With the REFLECTOR.

Thursday, September 14. 1704.

THE whole Nation seems overjoy'd at the Success of the *English* Arms abroad, and all the Corporations of *England* are following the Queen with Addresses of Congratulation, among the rest the City of *Norwich* sent up their Mayor, &c. To present their Address to Her Majesty, to express their Sense of the General Advantage: The Address may not be so remarkable for the Particulars as the unexpected Zeal of that particular City was for expressing their Acknowledgment.

A Fire happen'd this last Week in *Sturbridge* Fair, which burnt two or three of the Tradesmens Booths, and endanger'd the whole Fair, and put the People in a great fright, but was extinguished very happily by the diligence of the People, without any further damage.

The Man in whose Booth the Fire began was a Turner by Trade, and being Drunk and in Bed, tho' all his Goods were burnt, and his Booth on fire about him, he never wak'd till his Bed was on fire, and the Shirt burnt off of his back, at which he jumpt up and run thro' the fire and sav'd his life.

M   Some

Some Highway-News gives us occasion to warn the unwary not to carry too much Money about them on the Road.

Two *Leicestershire* Cheese Merchants having sold their Cheese at *Sturbridge* Fair, were Rob'd of above 150 Pounds between *Huntingdon* and one of the Countrymen was ill treated by the Highway-men, having parted with his Money with some Reluctance.

The REFLECTOR.

THE Address of the City of *N---ch* is not mentioned here for any thing remarkable in the wording it, but to vindicate that City from the Scandal laid upon it by a parcel of ill natur'd Whigs, who pretended that the *Jacobites* had such a powerful Influence upon the Citizens and Magistrates of that City, that they would not Address Her Majesty on that Occasion; that they would not dissemble so much as to wish Folks Joy of what they were not pleas'd, and to Congratulate the Government they would not pray for, they said was not honest.

But these Gentlemen have too much leave given them to talk Maliciously, the Business is founded on a meer Mistake. What if there are some *Jacobites* in the Court of Alder----n at *N---ch*? What if the Mayor be a Brewer, and there are seven Brewers Members of that Body, and six of them *Jacobites*, what's all this to the purpose? May not the Generality be Loyal and well disposed for all that? If Brewers are not proper to make Magistrates, the Lord have Mercy upon other Cities as well as *Nor---ch*.

After all, may not a *Jacobite* in Principle be a *Williamite* in Practice? Are there not thousands of the most Zealous Hearty *Jacobites* in the Nation that take the Oaths to the Queen? Can't a Man be a *Jacobite* and yet take the Oaths to the Government?

We find these Gentlemen are strangers to the thing, and do not really know what a *Jacobite* is, nor how many sorts of *Jacobites* there are.

Wherefore we think it not amiss to distinguish a little in this Case, and tell the World what a *Jacobite* is in the vulgar Acceptation of it.

An *English Jacobite*, is either,

1. A Man that having taken the Oaths to the late King *James*, thinks himself bound by that Oath to him and his Posterity, and that let the *Male Administration* of that Prince be what it will, they are still bound, and cannot with a safe Conscience comply with the present Government; and therefore tho' he lives quietly, and submits to the present Power, yet he cannot Swear to it, nor wish it well--and this meerly for a Principle of Conscience. This *Jacobite* may be, for ought we know a very honest Fellow, and we shall never censure his misinform'd Judgment.

As there is a Conventicle of such *Jacobites* openly held in the City of *N--ch*, we cannot think 'twas a Scandal to say these would not Address the Queens Majesty on the account of the Victory; for they cannot be glad of it, they cannot rejoyce at it, they do not pretend to be pleas'd with it, and they are too honest to dissemble in that case.

But

But we hope no Man will suspect us of a design to charge the Worshipful Mayor of *Norwich* with being one of this sort, we declare our selves of the Opinion that the Mayor of *Norwich* is not an h---t *Jacobite*.

The second sort of *Jacobites* is of those who tho' they heartily wish the Interest and Return of the late King *James*, and heartily pray for it when they chance to pray at all, yet at the same time make no scruple of the Oaths to the Government; as for former Oaths they don't trouble their Heads much about them, nor can they perswade themselves that Swearing to Princes signifies any thing, and therefore when they Swear to one Government they make nothing of Praying for another, of which Sir *W. Parkins* is a notable Instance, who Swore to K. *William*'s Government, but at the Gallows pray'd for King *James* as his only Lawful Prince.

'Tis a barbarous thing that these People should take upon them to charge the Mayor and Ald---n of *N---ch* with being of this sort of *Jacobites*; and therefore we are glad to see, not only that the City has made an Address, but that they have done it so forward and with so much diligence.

The further Conviction of this Truth appears from the Zeal and Diligence of those Loyal Gentlemen, for that the Mayor himself in Person, and one whole Member of the Court of Ald---n of that City came up on purpose.

Those that object against the Case, because no more of the Aldermen came up, are only a few ill-natur'd People that are out of Humour with People, because they think the Queen had not Honour enough done her in that Case. What have these People to do with, that if the Magistrates of *N---ch* had not thought it had been Honour enough to have their Mayor and a Committee of one Alderman appointed to wait on the Queen, they would without doubt have sent more.

And the Respect they shew'd the Queen was very plain in this, that notwithstanding there was 2 or 3 Ald---n of *N---ch* in Town here upon their private Affairs, yet the M---r thought fit not to desire them to accompany him thither, rather chusing to go as he came, than to dishonour Her Majesty with an appearance of Whiggish Aldermen.

Upon the whole of this Affair, 'tis very visible how well affected the whole City of *N---ch* is both in the Address, and in the Noble Deputation made to present it; and therefore we cannot but vindicate them from the Aspersions cast upon them in the best manner we can.

As to the *Jacobite* Conventicle at *Norwich*, as we have already noted such as them to be honest *Jacobites*. We hope the City of *Nor---ch* will suffer no Scandal upon that account; it is a good Principle not to disturb any body upon meer Principle of Conscience, and we cannot but own these are both the best sort, and the least dangerous to the Government.

Some have said that those only are the true Church of *England*, and that all the rest have abandon'd their Principles and are Schismaticks and Dissenters.

We shall not enter into the Debate of this Particular, at least not now; but this we cannot but allow that these of the two act from the best Principle, because they are what they seem; whereas the other, such as the six brewers of *N---ch*, and the like, pretend Loyalty to the Government, Swear to it, and at the same time countenance all the Enemies of the present Settlement, and are the Governments worst Enemies.

[44]

As being of this Principle, renders any Man's Character very black, so we hope the Address from the City of *Norwich* will clear the Mayor and Aldermen of that City from all possible Reflections of this sort, since they cannot in any manner of reason be suppos'd to be guilty of Signing such an Address, and at the same time retain thoughts of Jacobitism and Disaffection.

ADVERTISEMENTS.

A True State of the Difference between Sir Geo. Rook, Knt. and Will. Colepeper, Esq; Together with an Account of the Tryal of Mr. Nathanael Denew, Mr. Robert Britton, and Mr. John Merriam, before the Right Honourable Sir John Holt, Knt. Lord Chief Justice of England, on an Indictment for the Designs and Attempts therein mentioned against the Life of the said William Colepeper on Behalf of the said Sir George Rook.

The Locusts: Or, Chancery Painted to the Life, and the Laws of England Try'd in Forma Pauperis. A Poem.

B--ff--t B--sh--t: Or, the Fulness of More Plain English. In Two Sermons, for R--F--RM--T--N of M-N-N-RS.

An Elegy on the Author of the True-born Englishman; with an Essay on the late Storm.

The Wolf stript of his Shepherd's Cloathing. In Answer to a late Celebrated Book Intituled Moderation a Virtue; wherein the designs of the Dissenters against the Church: And their behaviour towards Her Majesty both in *England* and *Scotland* are laid open. With the Case of Occasional Conformity considered. Humbly offer'd to the consideration of Her Majesty, and her Three Estates of Parliament.

The New Association. Part II. With farther Improvements. As another and later Scots Presbyterian-Covenant, besides that mention'd in the former Part. And the Proceedings of that Party since. An answer to some Objections in the pretended *D. Foe*'s Explication, in the Reflections upon the Shortest Way, with Remarks upon both. Also an Account of several other Pamphlets, which carry on, and plainly discover the Design to Undermine and Blow-up the present Church and Government; particularly the Discovery of a certain Secret History, not yet Publish'd. With a short account of the Original Government. Compar'd with the Schemes of the Republicans and Whigs.

MDCCIV.

Numb. 13

THE
Master Mercury:

BEING

An ABSTRACT of the Publick NEWS

With the REFLECTOR.

Monday, September 18. 1704.

Among the various Additions to, and Fragments of News that our News-Writers have furnish'd us with in the absence of the Forreign Intelligence, this is the most remarkable, that Advice is come by a Ship that met a Vessel sent Express by Sir *G. Rook* of a great Engagement between the Confederate Fleet and the *French*, in which they tell us that 7 of the *English* and *Dutch* Fleet are lost, that the Fight has been very Bloody and Obstinate, that Admiral *Dilks* is kill'd or mortally wounded, that the *French* have lost one and thirty Men of War, and abundance of Men are kill'd on both sides, and that the *English* remain Victors, but that Sir *George Rook* has one Arm shot off, and one Leg.

But to set the Matter in a clearer Light, the following Particulars of that Engagement are brought by Captain *Trevor*, Commander of the *Triton*, who arrived here Express the 14th Instant, with Letters, dated *Aug.* 27. O. S. 1704.

On the 9th Instant, returning from Watering our Ships on the Coast of *Barbary* to *Gibraltar*, with little Wind Easterly, our Scouts to the Windward made the Signals of seeing the Enemy's Fleet, which, according to the Account they

they gave, confisted of 66 Sail, and were about 10 Leagues to the Windward of us. A Council of Flag Officers were called, wherein it was determined to lay to the *Eaftward* of *Gibralar* to receive and engage them; and our Fleet was ftrengthned with 1000 Marines which were in Garifon at *Gibraltar*; but perceiving that Night, by the Report of their Signal Guns, that they wrought from us, we followed them in the Morning with all the Sail we could make.

On the 11th we forced one of the Enemy's Ships a fhore near *Fuengirole*; the Crew quitted her, fet her on fire, and fhe blew up immediately. We continued ftill purfuing them; and the 12th, not hearing any of their Guns all Night, nor feeing any of their Scouts in the Morning, our Admiral had a Jealoufie they might make a double, and by the help of their Gallies flip between us and the Shore to the *Wefwards* fo that a Council of War was call'd, wherein it was refolved, That in cafe we did not fee the Enemy before Night, we fhould make the beft of our way to *Gibraltar*; but ftanding into the Shore about Noon, we difcovered the Enemy's Fleet and Gallies to the *Weftward* near Cape *Malaga*, going away large. We immediately made all the Sail we could after them, and continued the Chace all Night.

On *Sunday* the 13th, in the Morning, we were within three Leagues of the Enemy, who brought to with their Heads to the *Southward*, the Wind being *Eafterly*, formed their Line, and lay to receive us. Their Line confifted of 52 Ships, and 24 Gallies: They were very ftrong in the Center, and weaker in the Front and Rear; to fupply which, moft of the Gallies were divided into thofe Quarters: In the Center was Monfieur de Thouloufe with the White Sqadron; in the Van the White and Blue, and in the Rear the Blue; each Admiral had his Vice and Rear Admiral. Our Line confifted of 53 Ships; but the Admiral ordered the *Swallow* and *Panther*, with the *Lark* and *Newport*, and two Fire-fhips, to lie to the Windward of us, that in cafe the Enemy's Van fhould pufh thro' our Line with their Gallies and Firefhips, they might have given them fome Diverfion.

We bore down upon the Enemy in order of Battel till a little after 10 a Clock, when being about half Gun-fhot from them, they fet all their Sails at once, and feemed to intend to ftretch a head and weather us; fo that our Admiral was obliged to put the Signal out and begin the Battel, which was continued with very great Fury on both fides; but about two in the Afternoon the Enemy's Van gave way to ours, which was commanded by Sir *Cloudefly Shovell*, and led by Sir *John Lake*; as their Rear did to the *Dutch* towards Night; but their Body being very ftrong, and feveral of the Ships of the Admiral's, Rear-Admiral *Byng*'s, and Rear-Admiral *Dilkes*'s Divifions, being forced to go out of the Line for want of Shot, the Battel fell very heavy on the Admiral's own Ship, the *St. George* and the *Shrewsbury*: This want of Shot was occafioned by our Expence at *Gibraltar*; and tho' every Ship was fupplied to 25 Rounds two days before the Battel, which was judged fufficient, and would have been fo, if we could have got fo near the Enemy as the Admiral intended; yet every Ship that was on that Service wanted Ammunition before Night.

The Battel ended with the Day, when the Enemy went away by the help of their Gallies to the Leeward. In the Night the Wind fhifted to the *Northward*, and in the Morning to the *Weftward*, which gave the Enemy the Wind of us: We lay by all day within 3 Leagues of one another, repairing our

De-

Defects, and at Night they filed and stood to the *Northward*.

On the 15th in the Morning the Enemy was got 4 or 5 Leagues to the Windward of us; but a little before Noon we had a Breeze of Wind *Easterly*, with which we bore down on them till Four a Clock in the Afternoon; it being too late to engage, we brought to, and lay by with our Heads to the *Northward* all Night.

On the 16th in the Morning, the Wind being still *Easterly*, hazey Weather, and having no sight of the Enemy or their Scouts, we filed and bore away to the *Westward*, supposing they would have gone away for *Cadiz*; but being advised from *Gibraltar* and the Coast of *Barbary*, that they did not pass the *Streights*, we conclude they have been so severely treated, as to oblige them to return to *Toulon*, which may prevent any Attempt upon *Gibraltar* this Winter, or the sending any Succors, into *Cadiz*, the insulting the Coasts of *Portugal*, and constrain them to a Winter Passage to *West France*, if they intend any of their Ships thither this Year.

We have not yet the Particulars of the Enemy's Loss. The Marquis *de Villadarias* marching with his Army to Besiege *Gibraltar*, sent a Letter to the Prince of *Hesse*, Governor of that Place, that the *French* had burnt 8 of our Ships, taken 16, sunk 7; and he allows the *French* have lost 4 Men of War and one Gally, and that the Count *de Toulouse* is wounded. During the Action, we saw two of the Enemy's Gallies sink, and many of their Ships so disabled, that they were towed off by their Gallies, and we have reason to believe several of them perished; whereas there was not one of Her Majesty's Ships lost, and the *Dutch* lost only one called the *Albemarle*, of 64 Guns, which blew up by Accident the 16th in the Afternoon, after we had lost sight of the Enemy. We lost besides of the *English*, 695 Men killed, and had 1663 wounded, 150 of the latter on board the Admiral's own Ship, which for several Hours received the Fire of the *French* Admiral of 110 Guns, and of his two Seconds of 100 Guns each: We had also two Captains killed, and three wounded. Of the *Dutch*, Captain *Lunflager* was killed, and they had 400 Men killed and wounded.

The Battel is so much the more Glorious to Her Majesty's Arms, because the Enemy had a Superiority of 600 Great Guns; a Detachment having been made from our Fleet a few days before of Admiral *Vanderduffen* with 6 *Dutch* Men of War, and 4 of Her Majesty's Ships sent to the *Terceras*: The Enemy had likewise the Advantage of cleaner Ships, being lately come out of Port, and of being better provided with Ammunition, of which we had spent so great a store in the taking and furnishing of *Gibraltar*; not to mention the use they had of their Gallies in rowing on or off their great Ships: But all these Disadvantages were surmounted by the Bravery and good Conduct of our Officers, and the undaunted Courage of our Seamen.

The Admiral having left 2000 *English* Marines in *Gibraltar*, with a sufficient quantity of Stores and Provisions, and 48 Great Guns, besides one hundred that were in the Town before, the Season of the Year being far advanced, will return home with the great Ships, leaving behind him a strong Squadron for the Defence of the Coast of *Portugal*, which will likewise be in a readiness to succour *Gibraltar* if there should be occasion.

The REFLECTOR.

THE Death of the Champion of the *Camisars*, honest *Roland*, is mightily lamented in the World; all People give him the Character of a brave, a worthy, and a valiant Leader, but the *French* have taken him at an Advantage, and killed him as in our last Paper.

But the Cruelties of the *French* towards the Prisoners taken with this poor Man, has, as we are informed, so exasperated them on several Accounts, that they are now more desperate than ever, and have come to Resolutions of treating their Enemies the *French* in the same manner, if any of them shall fall into their Hands. Tis confess'd the *Camisars* have Reason for this Resolution; and the *French* may expect this Usage returned upon them if they go on with great odds: But it appears however, that though they were not to receive the like Treatment, yet they will lose this to their old Cause, that the Protestants are less bloody than the Papists.

These cruel Executions are seldom made use of on any Side, but they fill the People with the Abhorrence of such things in general, and of the Persons in particular, and there are innumerable Instances to be given, in which such Cruelties have driven People to such Desperation of Principles, that they may one time or other revenge it, and oftentimes they do so, as has been famously known in the Case of the Netherlands, and the King of *Spain* under the Duke *D'Alva*.

And what if this Cloud began in so small a Bulk as not to be valued, should be the great Cloud that should spread over the whole Horizon. The Reflections in the mean time are very seasonable and useful and just. The *Camisars*, it seems, on every Occasion shew themselves brave, and are never backward to signalize themselves; and if there was no such thing as an Obligation in Conscience, they deserve all the Honour and Acknowledgments from *Europe* that Protestants are able to give them.

We cannot but note here, that there has been a Scandal rais'd in this Case upon the Gentlemen concern'd in our late Government, that they discourag'd others from attempting the relief of the Camisars.

The Circumstances are plain, they pretend they are Rebels, that they have taken Arms against their Prince, that they may enjoy their Liberty, that they are ready to relieve all that are honest, but they put by this Cause because they think it is dishonourable.

Even these very Gentlemen think it very Honourable to assist the *Hungarian* Churches, they scruple nothing with them, they with them and their Posterity Success, and blame the Emperor for oppressing them.

But the *French* King has not opprest the *Camisars*, the Protestants have nothing at all to complain of, they are a People Industrious, and Diligent, and Obedient; and so far they are made use of; but for Oppression it cannot be considerable, there has always been more cry than hurt, they have made a noise of Persecution and Oppression, but they are Rebels, and Usurpers, and all the Oppression is but to take them from their Professions, and carry it on.

The defending the *Camisars* therefore must not be undertaken, they are Rebels, it may be of ill Consequence to our selves, &c. and other Nations may do the same.

MDCCIV.

[53]   Numb. 14

THE
Master Mercury:
BEING

An ABSTRACT of the Publick NEWS

With the REFLECTOR.

Thursday, September 21. 1704.

OUR last gave an Abstract of the Fight at Sea between the Confederate Fleet and the *French*.--- Since that we understand the former have thought fit to quit the *Mediteranean*, and are making the best of their way home.

Four Posts from *Holland* since that furnish us with a great variety of Particulars from abroad.

First, By the *Paris* Gazette of the 20th of *September*, we find the *French* Account of the Engagement at Sea, which differs very much from ours, and 'tis very hard to reconcile the Differences that appear in the two Relations.

And since our Business is not to prove which gives the justest Accounts, the Claims that both make to Victory, being very positive, we shall only relate some Passages in which they differ. Our *London* Gazette of the 19th relates the Fight, as in our last, and in that we find the following Particulars.

First, He calls it a Victory.

Secondly, he says this Battel was Glorious to Her Majesty's Arms, because of the Superiority of the Enemy, having 600 great Guns more than the *English*.

Thirdly, He says the Battel ended with the Day, when the Enemy went away.

O   Fourth-

(54)

Fourthly, He says, that on the 14th our Fleet and the Enemy lay by all day within 3 Leagues, repairing their Defects, and at Night the Enemy stood to the *Northward,* and tho' they had the Wind of us did not care to Engage.

Fifthly, He says that the next Day our Fleet having the Wind, bore down on the Enemy till 4 a Clock, but thought it too late to Engage, and so lay by all Night.

The next Day was Foggy, and not being able to see them we came away for *Gibraltar*; whether they slipt from us in the Fog, or we from them is left in doubt, for the Gazette is silent in the Case.

But all these Circumstances of Victory appearing, our Rejoycing has been very great on that Score.

To examine a little the *French* Account.

First, They tell us, that notwithstanding the Enemy had the Advantage of the Wind, they kept as close to the Wind as they could, while the Count *de Thoulouse* made all possible Efforts to come at them.

That the Marquiss *de Vallette* forced 5 of Sir *Cloudsly Shovell's* Squadron to quit the Line of Battel, and had entirely routed them but for the Bombs that disabled some of our Ships.

That the *English* sheer'd off, and ended the Fight in the Van about Five, the Center about Seven, and the Rear about Night.

That the next Day the *English* stood over to the Coast of *Barbary*, and were out of sight in the Evening.

The next Day they appear'd again, and having the Wind at *East*, had a fair Opportunity to Engage again, but did not think fit to approach.

And since that they have not been heard of, but 'tis supposed they have pass'd the *Straights*, and on the 27th the Count *de Thoulouse* return'd to *Malaga*.

And from *Paris* we are told *Te Deum* was Sung for the Victory.

The REFLECTOR.

GOD Almighty is the most oblig'd to these *Northern* Nations of any People in the World, they are the diligentest of all People to watch all Opportunities of Expressing their Gratitude and Thankfulness for Mercies that they oftentimes run the Risque of, thank him for nothing, rather than not thank him at all.

We are not to question but that we have had a great Victory, and if the Publick Prints had given no Accounts of the Particulars, we are free to declare 'tis as Signal a Victory as this Nation ever receiv'd.

No sooner was it read that we had not one Ship taken by the Enemy but we conclude it a Victory, and whereas Mr. *Observator* is very diligent to lessen the Greatness of it, we cannot but think it our Duty to make it plain to the World that it is a very great Victory, and one of the most Signal Mercies of God to this Nation that ever befel us, and ought to be remembred accordingly; and as this is a bold Undertaking, we shall attempt to make it out from the very words of the Publick Prints, Exhibited by Authority, and which there is all the Reason in the World to believe.

In the first place 'tis told us by our Gazette that there was not a Ship in the Confederate Fleet but wanted Ammunition before Night.

And

And was it not a Victory, that when the Confederate Fleet wanted Ammunition the *French* did not fall upon them and destroy them all; the *French* could not but perceive the want among us, and when some of our Ships were forc'd to Tow off for want of Shot, that was all one as so many Ships beaten, and why the rest were not beaten, if it be true that they wanted Shot, let them answer that know how.

But we had another Escape equal to this, and which must give the Title of Victory to the *English*, and that in a most extraordinary way.

Notwithstanding that all our Ships wanted Ammunition, as is before noted, yet on the next day but one we bore down upon the Enemy, but it was to late to Engage.

This was certainly a great piece of *English* Gallantry, no Nation in the World but the *English* could have Courage for such an Action, *strange Boldness!* to dare a whole *French* Fleet to Battle, and have neither Powder nor Shot on Board.

If this was not a Victory I know not what can deserve the name of it?

Here also we must observe how much the Case is alter'd in *England* in these few Years last past, we certainly, to our Comfort be it spoken, have fewer Traytors among us than before; for had it been discover'd to the *French* that we had spent all our Ammunition in the first Days Fight, it might have been but an ill Jest that we fac'd them next day, and we might have paid dear for it.

From hence also some Men argue that it could not have been true that our Ships wanted Ammunition, because we faced the Enemy's Fleet the next day; for tho' it was a Token of great Gallantry in our Admiral, yet perhaps some People may say there was but little Discretion in it. For,

1st One Traytor might have reveal'd it, and then all the Fleet had been undone.

2d. If the *French* had ventur'd to Fight again it would have reveal'd it self, *and still we had been ruin'd that way*, and they could not be certain the *French* would not come on.

3dly, Therefore they think it cannot be true that the Ships wanted Ammunition; for that our Admiral could never be guilty of an Indiscretion so great to hazard the Royal Navy with an Enemy in Fight, and neither Powder nor Shot on Board.

Besides here is an Article afterwards contradicts it, which says the Admiral furnish'd *Gibraltar* with Ammunition and Warlike Stores, which could not well be if he wanted for himself.

But then here is another Difficulty, that if they did not want Shot, &c. then those Ships which Tow'd out of the Line must be beaten out, and this mars our Victory; so that we are at a loss every way.

As to some other Contradictions which cannot be well reconcil'd, tho' they remain so 'tis no great matter.

As 1st, The Admiral and his two Seconds had the Enemy very heavy upon them, yet in another place it says could not get up so near them as he intended.

They fought till the Night ended the Battel, and then the Enemy went away. This is an odd Sea Phrase, and something unusual, and it remains undecided, whether they went on Horseback or on Foot.

They they tell us they went away, and yet they saw them again the next day, and the next to that in a Line of Battel.

The third day they bore down on the *French* till 4 a Clock, and then 'twas thought too late to Engage. Now our Opinion is plain in this Case, that they might

might have left out the words 4 a Clock, for 'twas certainly too late to Engage if they wanted Powder and Shot.

Upon the whole the Matter is much for the Advantage of *England*, and the *French* lost the day in losing so great an Opportunity of ruining the *English* Fleet, the like of which I hope they will never have again.

The next Crisis of this Action is the Fog, it seems both the Fleets were lost in this Fog, the *English* says they suppose the *French* are gone back to *Thoulon*, the *French* says they suppose the *English* are gone through the *Straights* Mouth, and this is the only Clause in which we think the *French* Account has the better of us; for their Guess it seems happens to be right, and ours wrong; for we were re-pais'd the *Streights*, and they were still in *Malaga* Road.

And this, if any thing is the ground the *French* have to call it a Victory, viz. that we left them the Place of Battel.

As to our seeking them to fight again, we cannot say any thing to it, we would not have it be true, whether it be or no, for we cannot wish the Enemy's of our Admirals should have it to say of him, that he shou'd put a Navy to such a hazard as to offer Batsel again when he had no Powder or Shot.

At last this Battel is welcome to *England*, whether it be a Victory or no. Now the *English* Admiral has told the World he knows when to fight as well as when to let it alone, and that when he comes to a Battel *English* Men will make good the Character given them by a famous Poet in a Poem call'd a *Hymn to Victory*.

Particularly the Nation makes good these two Lines of that Poem,

Let him but Fight, give but his Valour vent,
And if he's beaten, he's as well content.

Let it be how it will the Nation is glad there is a Battel, and let which side soever have the better in the Fight. It is a Victory that our Fleet is come safe off, and therefore we have more reason to sing *Te Deum* than the *French*.

ADVERTISEMENT.

A True State of the Difference between Sir Geo. Rook, Knt. and Will. Colepeper, Esq; Together with an Account of the Tryal of Mr. Nathanael Denew, Mr. Robert Britton, and Mr. John Merriam, before the Right Honourable Sir John Holt, Knt. Lord Chief Justice of England, on an Indictment for the Designs and Attempts therein mentioned against the Life of the said William Colepeper on Behalf of the said Sir George Rook.

The Locusts: Or, Chancery Painted to the Life, and the Laws of England Try'd in Forma Pauperis. A Poem.

B- ff--t B--fh--t: Or, the Fulness of More Plain English. In Two Sermons, for R--F--RM--T--N of M-N-N-RS.

An Elegy on the Author of the True-born English-Man; with an Essay on the late Storm.

MDCCIV.

[57]   Numb. 15.

The Master Mercury:

BEING

An ABSTRACT of the Publick NEWS

Monday, September 25. 1704.

THE News of our Fleet taking up the last Papers, we are obliged to come a little behind the Town with the rest of the Foreign Accounts.

The *French* have made great Rejoycings upon what they call a Victory at *Sea*; and this they the rather do, because they really wanted a pretence, to sing *Te Deum*, for something to keep up the Spirits of the People.

Our News from the Army, under the Duke of *Marlborough*, is very considerable. The *French* Army, under the Duke *de Villeroy*, had made a face of disputing, with the Confederates, the Passage of the Rivers between *Philipsbourg* and *Landau*, at *Germersheim*, the which is a very strong Pass. They had posted a good Body of Horse, and four *Swiss* Batallions, and had raised Batteries on a little River call'd the *Quiech*; but when they found the Confederates came on, and resolved to Attack them in these Strengths, they thought fit to Quit them all, and Retreat towards *Haguenau*, and from thence to *Strasburgh*.

However, in the interim of this, they failed not to put a large Garrison into *Landau*, furnishing it with all things necessary for a long Siege; and four Batalions were afterwards added to the Garrison, being convoy'd, together with a large Sum of Money, by the Duke de
Mar-

Monfort, Son-in-Law to the Duke *de Villeroy*; who being Attack'd on their return, by the *Huffars* of the Imperial Army, were entirely Defeated, and the said Duke being taken Prifoner, is fince dead of his Wounds.

Upon this Retreat of the *French*, the Confederates advanced, and Prince *Lewis* of *Baden*, who, under the King of the *Romans*, is to govern that Siege, Invefted the Place on the 12th of *September*, New Stile, and the Trenches were opened on the 16th.

The Duke of *Marlborough*, and Prince *Eugene* of *Savoy*, Cover the Siege, and are expected to March towards *Strasburgh*, where the *French* are making great Preparations to Defend themfelves, having raifed great Batteries in the Avenues to that Place, and fortifie the Paffes Night and Day.

The *French* Armies, under the Duke *de Villeroy*, and the Marefchal *Marfin*, are reckoned 40000 Men, tho' they give out themfelves to be 60000; but as the Garrifon of *Landau* has taken up 7000 Men, and the *Bavarian* and *French* Batalions, who came from the Battel, muft be very weak; they who call them 40000 are thought to be right, and fome fay their Horfe are in an ill Cafe, which makes them avoid Fighting with all poffible Care.

In the mean time, The Confederate Armies encreafe daily; and as Victory always heartens up the Parties, thofe Princes, who before were backward enough to fupply, are now fending more Men to come in for a fhare of the Succefs.

Ulm is Surrendered, after a Siege but of twelve Days open Trenches; the Garrifon obtain'd Honourable Conditions, and were Conducted to the Fort *Kiel* near *Strasburgh*.

The Booty found in this City is very great, all the *French* and *Bavarian* Train, and their heavy Cannon, being laid up here; and as they had neither Leifure nor Horfes to carry it off, the Confederates found 220 pieces of Brafs Cannon, 25 Mortars, 2000 Barrels of Powder, and abundance of fmall Arms.

From this Siege the General, Count *Thungen*, brings 20 Batalions and 12 Squadrons, to join the Confederates before *Landau*, leaving three Batalions in Garrifon at *Ulm*, and thefe joined with the Troops Pofted at *Rotwieler*, to Defend the Dutchy of *Wirtemburgh*, and with' the Troops in the Lines at *Stolhoften*, which are now flighted as ufelefs, and with the Duke of *Marlborough* make up the Confederate Army 105 Patallions, 220 Squadrons, exclufive of 10000 Men the Elector of Palatine is drawing together, and 6000 *Heffians*, who are preparing to join and Befiege the Caftle of *Traerbach*, which much incommodes both thofe Princes.

The King of the *Romans* is parted from *Vienna*, on his way to the Army, to fhare the Conquefts and Glory of this wonderful Campaign, and 'tis expected our next Advices will tell us he is arrived in the Camp before *Landau*, the Siege whereof will be carried on with the utmoft Vigour, and Batteries are preparing for 160 pieces of Cannon and 50 Mortars; and as this is a Force was never ufed before any Place in the World; 'tis thought impoffible the Town fhould hold out above 12 Days but it muft be torn in pieces, by the Violence of the Batteries.

All our Letters agree, the Duke of *Bavaria* has quitted the *French* Armies on the *Rhine*, and with his own Guards only, is gone for *Bruffels*. The King of *France*, to Comfort him, has Remitted him 100000 Piftoles to repair his Equipages, and furnifh his Court, and ordered all poffible Honours to be done him in his Paffage.

The Government of *Flanders* will be made Hereditary to him, and fome additional Honours given for the Reward of his Fidelity to *France*.

We

We have strange and wonderful News from *Poland*; all Men expected on the March of the King of *Sweden*, for *Lemberg*, a bloody Battel would ensue, and those that understood the Affairs of that Country, as few People did, were in in pain for King *Augustus*, lest the *Swedes* should force him to Fight, his *Saxon* Forces having not yet join'd him.

As the Fortune of the *French* Affairs seems to turn all on a suddain, so does that of their Allies. The first Blow the King of *Sweden* met with, on that side, was near *Posen*, where the *Saxon* Force, who were fetch'd from the *Danube*, and had been in *Saxony* to Recruit themselves, had march'd through *Prussia*, and been join'd with the Gentry of *Great Poland*, Attack'd the Party of the new King, on that side, and Defeated them, killing above 700 *Swedes*, and taking great numbers Prisoners, with all their Cannon and Baggage.

The King of *Sweden*, after having made a new King in *Poland*, was march'd away, with all his Army, to Attack, as it was given out, the King of *Poland*.

How he has manag'd his Affairs, on that Side, we cannot tell; but this we find, That the King of *Poland*, pretending to fly from the *Swedes*, as usual, made a Feint, and giving the *Swedes* a slip, has Countermarch'd of a suddain, and leaving 3000 Men about *Lemberg*, march'd down the *Vistula*, with 12000 Horse, directly for *Warsaw*.

The new King, with all the Relicks of the Confederacy that were with him, surprized by this unexpected March of the *Poles*, shifted every one for himself as the fright and hurry they were in would permit; some with their Wives and Children followed the Fortunes of their new King, and run away into *Prussia*; some one way, some another, and those that could not make their Escape, shut themselves up in the Castle, supposing this was but some flying March of the King of *Poland*'s Army, and that he would not stay to Besiege them.

But they found themselves mistaken, for King *Augustus* attackt the Town, and entred it immediately, where he took a vast Booty of the Horses and Equipages, Furniture and Stores, both of the *Swedes* and the Confederates, and made the City pay him 20000 Rix-dollars to exempt them from Destruction.

The Castle was forthwith Attack'd, and the Cannon brought before it, Batteries prepared, and all things made ready for an Assault, which the Garrison perceiving, and knowing their own Weakness, they surrendered at Discretion; and thus a great many of King *Augustus*'s principal Enemies are fallen into his Hands, particularly the Bishop of *Posen*, General *Horn*, the two *Swedish* Ambassadors, Monsieur *Palmquist*, and Monsi. *Wachtstager*, with near 100 Officers belonging to the *Swedes* and Confederate Forces, and about 800 *Swedish* Soldiers, besides *Poles*.

The King of *Poland* flusht with the Success is grown very strong. The *Saxon* Forces in *Great Poland* have taken the City of *Posnania* at Discretion, and are march'd to join their King, who has now with him 2500 *Saxon* Horse, 8000 *Saxon* Foot, 4000 *Polish* Horse, all Gentlemen; and 20000 *Cossacks*, besides the Army he left near *Lemberg* to face the *Swedes*, which consists of 10000 *Cossacks*, 18000 *Muscovite* Foot, 6000 *Saxon* Foot and 1000 *Saxon* Horse, and besides 12000 *Saxons* more which lye on the Frontiers of *Silesia*, ready to joyn on occasion, and who 'tis probable will now advance into *Poland*.

These Troops had Halted on the Frontiers by the Kings Order, because there was some Reason to fear the *Swedes* should attempt an Invasion of *Saxony* thro' the Dutchy of *Silesia*; but now 'tis thought that fear is over, the King Marches from *Warsaw* to join them, and then resolves to follow the *Swedish* Army, which

which will then be in some danger, having one Army before him, and another behind him, each of equal Force to his own.

While these things are doing, the *Swedish* Affairs go to wreck in *Livonia*; several Expresses are said to bring Advice that the Czar of *Muscovy* has taken the strong Town of *Narva* by Storm, but that contrary to the usual Custom of the *Muscovites*, the Czar himself ordered Quarter to be offered to the Garrison and so made them Prisoners of War.

As this is a considerable Conquest, and makes the *Muscovites* Master of a very considerable Province, Fruitful and Populous, so it has given him such a Port in the *Baltick*, as may in time make him as formidable by Sea as he begins to be by Land.

Upon the News of the taking of *Narva*, the Citizens of *Revel* are in a great Consternation; and they write from thence, That they have Advice that the *Muscovites* look that way already, and that they give out they will Attack *Revel* and *Riga* together, as they did before *Narva* and *Dorpat*.

From *Italy* we have an Account, That the Duke de *Vendosme* continues to press very hard upon the Duke of *Savoy*; That he has Invested *Ivrea*, and the Trenches had been opened about six Days; and the Advice from *Paris* says, he makes no question to reduce the Town in 12 Days more.

Yet notwithstanding all this, we are informed the Duke of *Savoy* has wrote to the Confederates, that he is in no fear of being push'd to any Extremities this Campaign, and only Sollicites to be so Reinforced as to be able to Act Offensively the beginning of the next, not doubting to retrieve all this in one successful Campaign.

The Approach of the *Germans*, under Count *Leinengen*, and Count *Guttenstein*, to the *Mantuan*, and the expectation the *French* have of a Storm on that side, has obliged the Duke de *Vendosme* already to send a Detachment of 1500 Horse to the Grand Prior, and that General has already raised the Blockade of *Mirandola* to strengthen his Army, which with these Additions, pretend now to be 18000 Men, besides the Garrisons in *Mantua*, *Ostiglia*, and other Posts on that side.

These Particulars of Forreign News are so many and so long, and so material, that we are obliged to Adjourn our Reflector till the next Paper.

ADVERTISEMENT.

A True State of the Difference between Sir Geo. Rook, Knt. and Will. Colepeper, Esq; Together with an Account of the Tryal of Mr. Nathanael Denew, Mr. Robert Britton, and Mr. John Merriam, before the Right Honourable Sir John Holt, Knt. Lord Chief Justice of England, on an Indictment for the Designs and Attempts therein mentioned against the Life of the said William Colepeper on Behalf of the said Sir George Rook.

The Locusts: Or, Chancery Painted to the Life, and the Laws of England Try'd in Forma Pauperis. A Poem.

B--ff--t B--sh--t: Or, the Fulness of More Plain English. In Two Sermons, for R--F--RM--T--N of M-N-N-RS.

MDCCIV.

WILLIAM ANDREWS CLARK
MEMORIAL LIBRARY

UNIVERSITY OF CALIFORNIA, LOS ANGELES

The Augustan Reprint Society

PUBLICATIONS IN PRINT

The Augustan Reprint Society

PUBLICATIONS IN PRINT

1948-1950

16. Henry Nevil Payne, *The Fatal Jealousie* (1673).
18. "Of Genius," in *The Occasional Paper*, Vol. III. No. 10 (1719), and Aaron Hill, *Preface to The Creation* (1720).
19. Susanna Centlivre, *The Busie Body* (1709).
22. Samuel Johnson, *The Vanity of Human Wishes* (1749), and two *Rambler* papers (1750).
23. John Dryden, *His Majesties Declaration Defended* (1681).

1951-1953

26. Charles Macklin, *The Man of the World* (1792).
31. Thomas Gray, *An Elegy Wrote in a Country Churchyard* (1751), and *The Eton College Manuscript*.
41. Bernard Mandeville, *A Letter to Dion* (1732).

1964-1965

110. John Tutchin, *Selected Poems* (1685-1700).
111. *Political Justice* (1736).
113. T. R., *An Essay Concerning Critical and Curious Learning* (1698).

1965-1967

115. Daniel Defoe and others, *Accounts of the Apparition of Mrs. Veal* (1705, 1706, 1720, 1722).
116. Charles Macklin, *The Covent Garden Theatre* (1752).
117. Sir Roger L'Estrange, *Citt and Bumpkin* (1680).
120. Bernard Mandeville, *Aesop Dress'd or a Collection of Fables* (1740).
124. *The Female Wits* (1704).

1968-1969

133. John Courtenay, *A Poetical Review of the Literary and Moral Character of the Late Samuel Johnson* (1786).
136. Thomas Sheridan, *A Discourse Being Introductory to His Course of Lectures on Elocution and the English Language* (1759).
137. Arthur Murphy, *The Englishman from Paris* (1756).

1969-1970

138. [Catherine Trotter] *Olinda's Adventures* (1718).
139. John Ogilvie, *An Essay on the Lyric Poetry of the Ancients* (1762).
140. *A Learned Dissertation on Dumpling* (1726) and *Pudding and Dumpling Burnt to Pot or a Compleat Key to the Dissertation on Dumpling* (1727).

141. Sir Roger L'Estrange, Selections from *The Observator* (1681-1687).
142. Anthony Collins, *A Discourse Concerning Ridicule and Irony In Writing* (1729).
143. *A Letter From a Clergyman to His Friend, with an Account of the Travels of Captain Lemuel Gulliver* (1726).
144. *The Art of Architecture, A Poem* (1742).

1970-1971

145-146. Thomas Shelton, *A Tutor to Tachygraphy, or Short-writing* (1642) and *Tachygraphy* (1647).
147-148. *Deformities of Dr. Samuel Johnson* (1782).
149. *Poeta de Tristibus: or the Poet's Complaint* (1682).
150. Gerard Langbaine, *Momus Triumphans: or the Plagiaries of the English Stage* (1687).

1971-1972

151-152. Evan Lloyd, *The Methodist. A Poem* (1766).
153. *Are These Things So?* (1740), and *The Great Man's Answer to Are These Things So?* (1740).
154. Arbuthnotiana: *The Story of the St. Alb-ns Ghost* (1712), and *A Catalogue of Dr. Arbuthnot's Library* (1779).
155-156. A Selection of Emblems from Herman Hugo's *Pia Desideria* (1624), with English Adaptations by Francis Quarles and Edmund Arwaker.

1972-1973

157. William Mountfort, *The Life and Death of Doctor Faustus* (1697).
158. Colley Cibber, *A Letter from Mr. Cibber to Mr. Pope* (1742).
159. [Catherine Clive] *The Case of Mrs. Clive* (1744).
160. [Thomas Tryon] *A Discourse ... of Phrensie, Madness or Distraction* from *A Treatise of Dreams and Visions* [1689].
161. Robert Blair, *The Grave. A Poem* (1743).
162. [Bernard Mandeville] *A Modest Defence of Publick Stews* (1724).

1973-1974

163. [William Rider] *An Historical and Critical Account of the Lives and Writings of the Living Authors of Great Britain* (1762).
164. Thomas Edwards, *The Sonnets of Thomas Edwards* (1765, 1780).
165. Hildebrand Jacob, *Of the Sister Arts: An Essay* (1734).
166. *Poems on the Reign of William III* [1690, 1696, 1699, 1702].
167. Kane O'Hara, *Midas: An English Burletta* (1766).
168. [Daniel Defoe] *A Short Narrative History of the Life and Actions of His Grace John, D. of Marlborough* (1711).

1974-1975

169-170. Samuel Richardson, *The Apprentice's Vade-Mecum* (1734).
171. James Bramston, *The Man of Taste* (1733).
172-173. Walter Charleton, *The Ephesian Matron* (1668).
174. Bernard Mandeville, *The Mischiefs That Ought Justly to be Apprehended From a Whig-Government* (1714).
174X. John Melton, *Astrologaster* (1620).

1975-1976

175. *Pamela Censured* (1741).
176. William Gilpin, *Dialogue upon the Gardens . . . at Stowe* (1748).
177. James Bramston, *Art of Politicks* (1729).
178. James Miller, *Harlequin-Horace or the Art of Modern Poetry* (1731).
179. [James Boswell] *View of the Edinburgh Theatre during the Summer Season, 1759* (1760).
180. Satires on Women: Robert Gould, *Love Given O're* (1682); Sarah Fige, *The Female Advocate* (1686); and Richard Ames, *The Folly of Love* (1691).

Publications of the first eighteen years of the society (numbers 1 - 108) are available in paperbound units of six issues at $16.00 per unit, from Kraus Reprint Company, Route 100, Millwood, New York 10546.

Publications in print are available at the regular membership rate of $5.00 for individuals and $8.00 for institutions per year. Prices of single issues may be obtained upon request. Subsequent publications may be checked in the annual prospectus.

Make check or money order payable to

T̲h̲e̲ R̲e̲g̲e̲n̲t̲s̲ o̲f̲ t̲h̲e̲ U̲n̲i̲v̲e̲r̲s̲i̲t̲y̲ o̲f̲ C̲a̲l̲i̲f̲o̲r̲n̲i̲a̲

and send to

The William Andrews Clark Memorial Library
2520 Cimarron Street, Los Angeles, California 90018